AROUND 1700:
CARRIERS AND TRAVELLERS

A By river and sea – moving freight
B Highways and by-ways – road conditions through the eyes of Celia Fiennes
C Good and bad ways – road conditions and road repairs
D Long distance transport – heavy goods by land
E Skills section: sources

Leading products, 1700

One horse could pull

On soft roads	⅛ ton
On hard roads	¼ ton
On wooden rails	2 tons
On rivers	30 tons

From London by fastest coach, in summer

To Bath	50 hours
To Norwich	50 hours
To Manchester	98 hours

Before you read on, how do you think:

a) Pottery reached Plymouth from around Stoke on Trent?
b) A traveller from the south would visit relatives in Carlisle?
c) A letter from London arrived in York?
d) Wool from Yorkshire sheep reached weavers in Norwich?

In 1700 the time was long past when farmers and farm labourers grew food only for their own use. The map on page 1 shows that most districts had specialised farm products which were sold all over the country. There were also manufacturing specialities. Hardly a family in Britain took no part in manufacturing. It might be just the women and children who span wool into thread, made lace or plaited straw, but men often worked as weavers or did other textile work in winter. In other places they combined owning a few sheep or cattle with making nails, chairs or farm tools. In many parts they mined for coal, lead or copper, dug salt from the ground or quarried the stones needed for millstones in the corn mills which dotted the countryside.

A merchant with corn, cheese, wool, coal or nails to sell had to decide on the best route for his produce. Bulky or very heavy goods started off on carts, waggons or even sledges. Usually this first stage went only to the nearest sea or river port. It was much cheaper to send goods by water unless they ran the risk of getting damaged or going bad on the slow journey. A lot of the finer cloths made in Yorkshire, for instance, were sent all the way to London by packhorse. Fishermen at Hastings sent 320 packhorse-loads of fish each day to London because this journey took fifteen hours while the sea route took up to two days. Where speed and damage were not problems the aim was to get goods to water as quickly as possible.

The map on page 1 shows the rivers that were navigable, which meant the water could be used by barges carrying thirty or forty tonnes. It also shows a few of the 300 or more towns that were inland ports in 1700.

Freight in the west

The River Severn was the great trading highway in the west. Goods from North Wales, the Lancashire cloth districts and the Staffordshire potteries were put on barges at Shrewsbury. Bewdley was the port for midlands ironware and Shropshire coal. At Worcester salt came by packhorse from Droitwich, seven miles away, at a cost of 15s a ton. The seventy-seven-mile journey down the Severn to Bristol cost 5s a ton.

The Severn barges were known as trows. They had sails which could only be used when there was enough wind. A bargemaster was in charge for the whole journey and sometimes owned the trow himself. For each stretch he would take on a gang of labourers known as halers who tugged the trow along, sometimes with the help of horses. The cargoes ended their river journey at Gloucester or Bristol. Some were transferred to barges which went up the River Wye into Wales and others to sea-going ships which carried them to Europe, Africa or the Americas. The largest amounts were loaded onto sailing ships which took them to other British ports.

A

A1 A view of Gloucester. An engraving by J Kip, 1712.

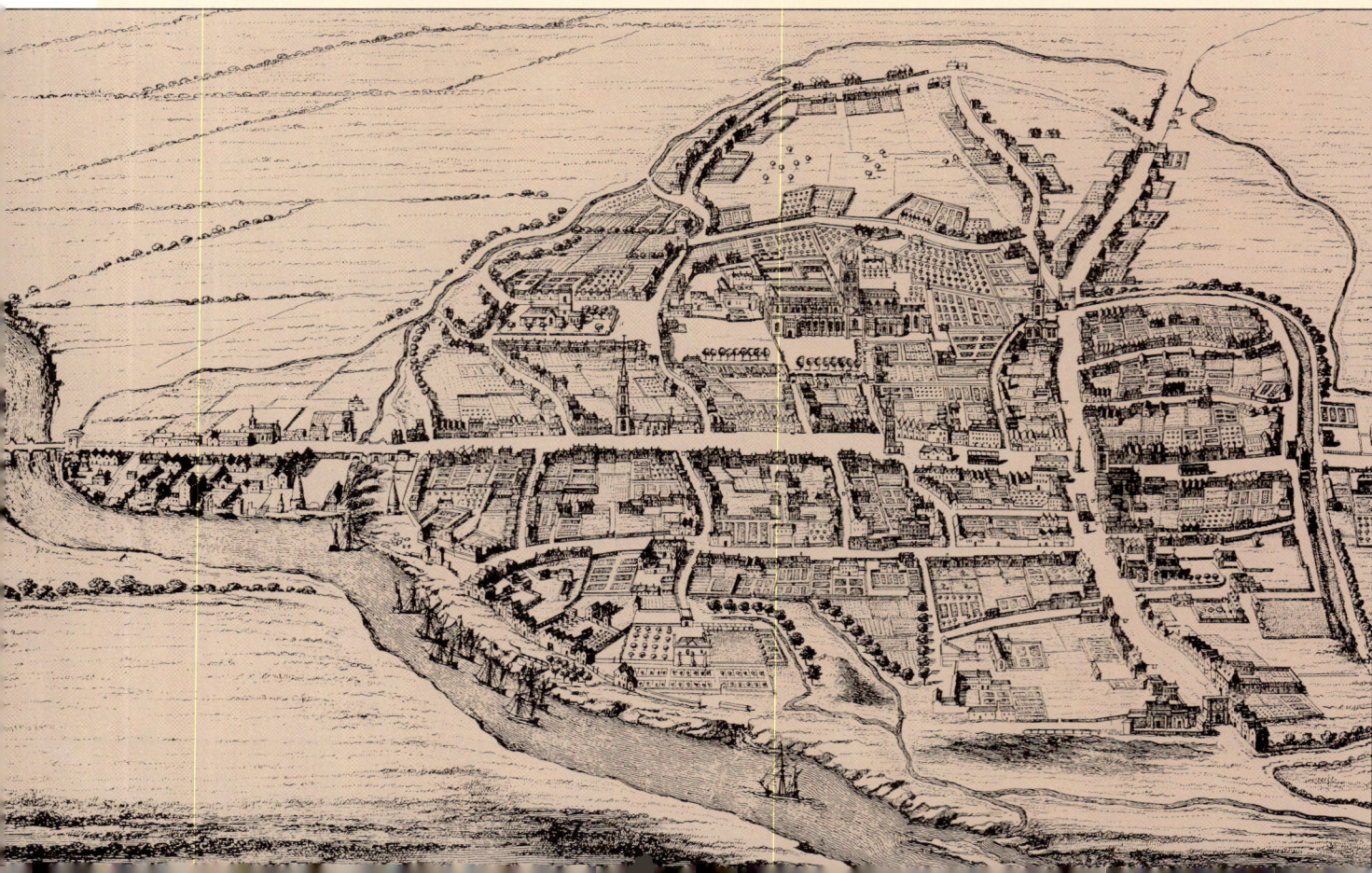

A2 In 1698 Celia Fiennes was completing her 'great journey' around England on horseback. One place she visited was Gloucester.

> Here is a very large good Key on the river; they are supply'd with coales by the shipps and barges which makes it plentifull, they carry it sledgs thro' the town, its the great Warwickshire coale I saw unloading

Celia Fiennes, *My Great Journey*, 1698

1. Where, in the picture, do you think the quay seen by Celia Fiennes was most likely to be?
2. Along which water route would the coal have travelled?

Freight in the east

On the other side of the country the Severn's rival was the Trent which carried a great variety of goods; pottery from Staffordshire, iron from the west midlands, stockings from the east midlands, grindstones from the Derbyshire hills, and grain from Lincolnshire.

B

Bawtry was connected with the Trent by the River Idle. Daniel Defoe described Bawtry's trade.

> By this navigation, this town of Bawtry becomes the centre of all the exportation of this part of the country, especially for heavy goods, which they bring down hither from all the adjacent countries, such as lead, from the lead mines and smelting-houses in Derbyshire, wrought iron and edge-tools, of all sorts, from the forges at Sheffield . . .
>
> Also millstone and grindstones in very great quantities are brought down and shipped off here and so carry'd by sea to Hull, and to London, and even to Holland also. This makes Bawtry Wharf be famous all over the south part of the West Riding of Yorkshire, for it is the place where all their heavy goods are carried, to be embarked and shipped off.

Daniel Defoe, *A Tour Thro' the Whole Island of Britain*, 1724–7

3. With the help of the map on page 1 make a sketch to show Bawtry's links with manufacturing in its hinterland.
4. In which way was Bawtry a different sort of port from Shrewsbury or Bewdley?

Sailing the coasts

Defoe shows that some ships sailed up or across the North Sea into Bawtry. There were more ports for sea-going ships on the east coast of England than the west. Three of them, Hull, King's Lynn and Yarmouth were vital to the food supplies of London and other towns because each year they handled 1,000 ship-loads of corn grown in East Anglia and Lincolnshire.

The biggest ships were the colliers which left Newcastle or other places on the River Tyne with 'sea coal'. More than three-quarters ended up at coal wharves on the banks of the Thames in London.

C

On the Tyne. Waggons ran downhill under their own weight and the coal was delivered to barges, known as keelies, which carried the coal out to ships which took it to London. The wagons were then pulled back up the slope by horses.

5. Explain how this scene could be used to illustrate the main features of goods transport around 1700.

D

Coastal shipping was a vital part of the country's transport system right through the eighteenth century. In 1785 the Derby Mercury printed this notice:

GAINSBRO' SHIP NEWS.
ARRIVED.—The Supply, George Hickfon, with Groceries, &c. from London.—Mary, James Ballaſt; Choice, Robert Pinder; and Gainſbro', Robert Forbes, with Flint, from Gravefend.—Unit, John Popplewell, with Chalk from ditto.—And Tradeſgoodhope, Thomas Wall, with Wool, from Colcheſter.
SAILED.—The Derby, Francis Woodhoufe; and Eagle, James Wharam, with Nails, Crates, &c. for London.—And Sally, William Woolfey, with Cheefe, &c. for Colcheſter.

6. Why might readers in Derby be interested in this news?
7. What does the range of goods tell you about the coastal shipping trade?

B HIGHWAYS AND BY-WAYS

Between about 1590 and 1611 Shakespeare wrote thirty-seven plays. The word 'road' appeared in only one. People of that time kept to the old word 'way', and spoke of 'highways' for routes which made their way between larger towns and 'by-ways' which wandered off to the small villages and lonely farms.

'Road' came into use in the later seventeenth century as the word to describe the route you would take along the highways from one town to another. It was linked to 'ride' and in most people's minds it was connected with a journey that could be made on horseback.

In the 1690s Celia Fiennes travelled on many of these roads, and noted what she saw in her journals. She was the daughter of a colonel who had fought for Oliver Cromwell and the family had many connections among businessmen and landowners around the country. Celia made her journeys on horseback with two or three horses and a servant. Her most adventurous travel was the 'the great journey' in 1698. Most of her journals were taken up with descriptions of the towns and country houses she visited. But very often she made a comment about the difficulties, or even dangers, of road travel.

1. Note down the numbers of the comments which
   a) describe easy travelling,
   b) are critical of the roads,
   c) deal with carrying goods,
   d) describe the dangers and costs of road travel.

2. a) how would a traveller of this time describe a good road?
   b) what were the two main complaints about road conditions?
   c) what were the main ways of carrying goods on roads?
   d) what would be wise precautions for a road traveller to take?

① [In East Anglia]: the roade lay under water which is very unsafe for strangers to pass, by reason for the holes and quick sands and loose bottom.

Thence I went to Windham [Wymondham] . . . mostly on a Causey, the country being low and moorish and the road on the Causey was in many places full of holes, tho' it is secured by a barr at which passengers pay a penny a horse in order to the mending the way, for all about is not to be rode upon unless it is a very dry summer.

② [At Ely] the roads were full of water even quite to the town . . . I never saw a bitt of pitching in the streetes so its a perfect quagmire the whole Citty.

. . . this bridge was in the water, one must pass thro' water to it, and so beyond it a good way, and the road was so full of holes and quick sands I durst not venture . . . but I rather chose to ride round and ferry over in a boate (2 pence a horse).

③ ...to the City of Peterborough in Lincolnshire which was five long miles, the wayes deep and full of sloughs.

④ ...to Wiggon [*Wigan*] mostly in lanes and some hollow wayes, and some pretty deep stony way so forced us upon the high Causey.

⑤ ...to Lancaster town, I passed through an abundance of villages...mostly all along lanes being an enclosed country; they have one good thing...that at all cross wayes there are Posts with Hands pointing to each road with the names of the great town or market place that it leads to.

⑥ [*the Lake District*] They reckon it but 8 miles from the place I was at the night before but I was 3 or 4 hours at least going it; here I found a pretty good smith to shooe the horses, for these stony hills and wayes pulls off a shooe presently and wears them as thinn that it was a constant charge to shooe my horses every 2 or 3 dayes...

⑦ As I drew nearer and nearer to Newcastle I met with and saw an abundance of little carriages with a yoke of oxen and a pair of horses together, which is to convey the Coales from the pitts to the barges on the river.

[*From Newcastle*]...thence I proceeded a most pleasant gravell road on the ridge of the hill.

⑧ ...to Darlington which is a good way, but by the way I lost some of my nightcloths and little things in a bundle that the guide I hired carry'd.

⑨ [*Near Warrington*]...I went a very pleasant roade much on the Downs mostly champion ground.

⑩ [*Near Chester*]...2 fellows all on a suddain from the wood fell into the road, they look'd trus'd up with great coates and as it were bundles about them which I beleive was pistolls, but they dogg'd me one before the other behind and would...justle my horse out of the way to get between one of my servants horses and mine...but the Providence of God order'd it as there was men at work in the fields haye making.

⑪ From Worcestor we pass'd a large stone bridge over the Severn on which were many Barges that were tow'd up by the strength of men 6 or 8 at a tyme.

⑫ Glocester town lyes all along the banks of the Severne...its a low moist place therefore one must travel on Causeys which are here in good repaire...

⑬ ...passed thro' Kingswood and was met with a great many horses passing and returning loaden with coals just dug thereabouts.

⑭ ...to Taunton through lanes full of stones and, by the great raines just before, full of wet and dirt.

⑮ [*Cornwall*] Here indeed I met with more inclosed ground and soe had more lanes and a deeper clay road, which by the raine the night before had made it very dirty and full of water ...here my horse was quite down in one of these holes full of water but by the good hand of God's Providence...giving him a good strap he flounc'd up againe...

⑯ [*Exeter to Honiton*], all fine gravell way, the best road I have met withall in the West...

[*Exe to Chudleigh*] – the lanes are full of stones and dirt for the most part, because they are so close [*narrow*] the sun and wind cannot come at them, soe that in many places you travel on Causeys which are uneven also for want of a continued repaire.

⑰ [*from London to Ware*] thence to Hitching [*Hitchin*], most in lanes and deep land; in the winter bad roads.

⑱ Just by Lime you cross a little brooke into Devonshire – inclosures that makes the wayes very narrow, so as in some places a Coach and Waggons cannot pass; they are forced to carry their Corn and Carriages on horse backes with frames of wood like pannyers on either side the horse.

⑲ ...thence to Nottingham town and we ferried over the Trent, which is in some places so deep but waggons and horses ford it.

⑳ ...thence to York and so to Tadcaster. I observe that the ordinary people...in the northern parts can scarce tell you how farre it is to the next place and they tell you it is a very good gate, instead of saying it is a good way... in generall they live much at home and scarce ever go 2 to 10 miles from thence.

Celia Fiennes, *Journals*, 1698

Celia Fiennes's comments tie up with most other travellers of the time. All agreed that a good road was on higher ground, better still if it was gravelly. It was best if it passed through open countryside or 'champion' land which had not been divided into enclosed fields with hedges or walls. Champion land was even more important when travelling on the low roads because you could leave the main track and skirt round potholes, mud or ruts made in dried clay. This meant that you were passing through open fields with corn growing; straying riders or waggons were hated by farmers as much as modern ramblers who do not keep to footpaths.

In many places the road became a holloway. It had been worn down so much by horses and carts that it was lower than the ground on each side. Then the foot passenger or the horse rider would take to the 'causey' or causeway which might be two metres up. With luck the causey would have been paved at some time and you might be able to pick your way along the stones, even if they were broken and uneven.

To Celia Fiennes, the most difficult roads were those which followed a lane between enclosed fields. The lane would be a holloway but the hedge or wall would mean there was no causey. The way was usually bumpy, muddy and so narrow that there would no be room for a horse rider and cart to pass. You could easily get lost in the network of lanes. In 1697 Parliament passed a law ordering sign posts to be set up where lanes and roads met. Celia Fiennes saw some of the first in the narrow lanes north of Kendal.

A

1. Explain how each of these recent photographs can help to illustrate eighteenth-century travel conditions.

Travellers

Celia Fiennes could not possibly have made her great journey by coach. In 1698, and for thirty or more years after, horseback was the only way for a private traveller to travel except on half a dozen roads out of London. Few men from the wealthy classes did this and almost no women. Regular riders such as merchants' agents and judges or lawyers going between assizes could be recognised by their long thigh boots which protected them against the mud and water.

Perhaps the most common riders seen on the roads were the post-boys (although some were older men). The General Post Office dated back to the 1650s and by 1700 there was a network of post roads all leading to London and cross roads which linked them. London and the larger towns had post-offices where letters could be handed in and paid for in advance according to

A1 A well preserved causey near Penistone in Yorkshire

A2 A holloway on the route from Sheffield into Derbyshire. It was used by carts into the twentieth-century.

the distance they would travel. The working of the system depended on the post-houses (which were often inns) on the main post roads and the cross roads.

The post-house keeper took in mail which would be collected by local people, but his main job was to provide a change of horses for the post-boy. The General Post Office paid keepers a yearly sum for doing this, but they also had the sole right to provide a change of horses for private travellers. No-one travelling more than twenty miles or so used their own horse. They simply travelled between post-houses and changed their mount at each one.

Some wealthy families were beginning to own carriages but often the only good roads were those through the parklands around their country home. Carriage travel was uncomfortable and men often rode horses while the women tried to keep their balance inside a wildly lurching vehicle. Stage coach services had begun, but they were just as uncomfortable. Most services started in London. The ones which ran as often as two or three times a week only went as far as Bristol or Norwich – and both these were two-day journeys. A few weekly services ran up to a few towns in the midlands and the north. In winter, coach journey times were up to half as long again as in the summer.

Repairs

Long distance roads are usually in good condition only if the government takes charge of caring for them. The last rulers of Britain who saw the need for a country-wide system were the Romans. Their main reason for occupying Britain was to bring its peoples under control and to defend a northern frontier of their empire along Hadrian's Wall. After the Romans left, their network of roads was neglected for a thousand years.

In the sixteenth century, the Tudor monarchs tried to organise a country-wide highway system. Instead of taking direct charge, they passed the responsibility on to the parishes. Originally a parish had been simply a part of the countryside, served by a church and a priest. Under the Tudors it also became a 'civil parish' with responsibilities for local matters such as law and order, the care of the poor – and highways. All the rate-payers in the parish met at a vestry meeting and elected unpaid officials from among themselves. The most important were a Constable, an Overseer of the Poor and two Waywardens.

The duties of the Waywardens were laid down in the Highways Act of 1555 (and some additions in another Highways Act of 1563). Three times a year, they had to survey all the highways and bridges in the parish and report on repairs needed. The work was to be done by parishioners. Every farmer had to supply two of his labourers with oxen or horses and tools to work on the roads for six days each year. Landless labourers had to give six days free labour themselves.

Its not difficult to imagine the problems. No-one wanted to be an unpaid Waywarden. In most parishes the by-ways between local fields and houses were more important than the highways for passers-through. Farmers sent their labourers when they were not needed in the fields, which was more likely to be in the winter. The labourers themselves were not willing workers and there were many reports of the six days becoming little more than a holiday which worked to the profit of ale-house keepers.

B

An early eighteenth century painting of a road, by Amelia Long (1762–1837).

2. How does this painting illustrate the difficulties of making a national highway system?

Packhorses

Daniel Defoe had been a merchant before he turned novelist and wrote *Robinson Crusoe*. In the 1720s he published a travel book based on his many years of travelling and trading around Britain. In it he described the great fair at Stourbridge in Cambridgeshire where merchants from London came to buy goods from all over the country. One section traded in woollen goods from Lancashire and Yorkshire:

A

vast quantities of Yorkshire cloths, kerseys, penistons, cottons &c with all sorts of Manchester ware, fustians and things made of cotton wool; of which the quantity is so great, that they told me there were near a thousand horse-packs of such goods from that side of the country.

D. Defoe, *A Tour Thro' the Whole Island of Great Britain*, 1724–6

At the other end of the country we can find an advertisement for the sale of a packhorse team in Kendal which was one of the centres for packhorse owners in the north of England.

B

A Gang of Good Packhorses, containing eighteen in number...being one of the ancient Gangs which have gone with goods from York, Leeds and Wakefield to London.

C

1. Explain how you would identify one of these as a packhorse route and the other as a drover's road.

    C1   In Edale in Derbyshire. A painting by W.B. Gardener, 1908.
    C2   In North Wales.

Packhorses were the most usual form of long distance carriage for goods that did not go by water. They travelled in teams of about eighteen or twenty. The horses had a pannier on each side which made them just about narrow enough to pass through the lanes and holloways. Packhorse bridges needed to be built with low parapets so that the panniers could overhang. One or two men were enough to lead the string which travelled nose-to-tail announcing their coming by the bells on the horses' collars. Many of the packhorse trails and bridges can still be seen in the hilly countryside. But packhorses also travelled along the highways which have become tarmac roads. Part of the routes can sometimes be spotted by the name of a pub such as 'Packhorse' or 'Woolpack'.

As well as the long distance routes there were shorter trails, such as the saltways. The busiest went in all directions from the two main salt-producing districts – in south Cheshire and around Droitwich in Worcestershire. It was an ancient trade which has given many place-names to the countryside. On just one saltway from Middlewich to Sheffield you can find Salter's Flatt, Saltergate, Salter Lane and Salter Furlong as well as three stream crossings still called Saltersford.

Drovers

Meat could not be carried far by cart, horse or boat. It had to be taken on the hoof to the butcher who slaughtered the animal when he was ready to sell the carcass. Meat cattle mostly started life on the mountains of Wales and Scotland, and were brought to market by drovers. Each year tens of thousands of cattle were

driven at about ten miles a day towards London and the other towns in the southern half of England.

In the hilly districts, drove-roads were separate from packhorse trails. The packhorses with their surer feet could pick the shortest way along narrow highways and by-ways. Drove-roads had to meander round sides of hills, in open country where the cattle could graze as they went. When they came to any lowland road which had stones or paving, the cattle had to be shod by smiths who specialised in making split shoes, one for each part of the cloven hoof.

The leader of a droving team could be in charge of several hundred cattle worth several thousand pounds, which he would have to carry back to the farmer or the merchant. Quite often drovers became dealers themselves and bought the cattle which they led into England to sell. The largest number of droves ended up in Smithfield market in London. Fully-grown beasts went straight to a cattle fair near London. Here they were sold and kept a few weeks to be fattened after the long walk before being taken the last few miles to the slaughterhouse. Younger cattle walked from Scotland into the Lake District, or from Wales into the English midlands. There they were bought by farmers who specialised in fattening cattle before they went, with another drover, on the second leg of their journey.

There were also sheep droves, but the distances were usually shorter because many animals intended to end up as mutton were kept on the downs and heaths of south England. Pigs were driven to market but in smaller numbers because they were raised all over the country and many were kept in towns anyway. A specialism in Norfolk was fattening geese and turkeys. They, too, walked to London. Many were first driven through a patch of tar and then one of sand so that they were fitted with a primitive kind of boot.

Wheeled vehicles

Every district had its own design of cart which had developed to suit the local conditions and was used only locally. The only country-wide wheeled goods vehicle was the heavy clumsy waggon pulled by eight horses. Like the stage-coach, most of the waggon services were based in London and did most of their business in the south of England. Yet towns such as Manchester, Sheffield and Derby had a few waggons arriving each week. The waggon was useful for carrying a mixture of general goods and parcels which could be left at one of the inns on the route to be collected by the waggoner or by the person it was addressed to.

Waggons were unpopular with other road users. Most of them followed the main highways which were also the post-roads used by riders and they did a great deal of damage. The worst problems were on the stretches of road just north of London, especially on the Great North Road and Watling Street which went to Chester and North Wales. (Many parts of these roads are still under the tarmac of the A1 and A5). The land here was clay, and the horses and wheels churned this up, often making huge pot holes which deepened with every rainfall.

D

From Ralph Thoresby's diary, about 1700.

> rain had raised the washes upon the roads near Ware to the height that passengers from London that were upon the road swam, and a poor higgler [*peddlar*] was drowned, which prevented me travelling for many hours.
>
> R. Thoresby, *Diaries*

E

A picture showing how stones from the quarries on Portland island (used for many of the great eighteenth-century country houses) were carried on locally-made carts and sledges. The horses behind acted as brakes on the down slopes.

2. How does this illustrate the statement that 'each district had its own design of cart'?
3. How might the stone have reached builders putting up a country house near York or near Oxford?

9

Sources

The account of traditional ways of travel and transport has been supported by a selection of different kinds of sources. Some come from the years around 1700 while some are recent pictures of remains.

Complete this chart to show the range of sources you have studied in Part One.

Type of source   *Examples*

Diaries and letters from around 1700

Travel books from around 1700

Artist's impressions around 1700

Photographs showing evidence on the ground

Paintings showing evidence on the ground

Maps based on research by historians

Advertisements

Unsupported information

You have also been expected to take a lot of information on trust without any source. Find an example of this from each of 1A and 1D and say for each whether you think it is reasonable or not to accept what you are told.

Knowledge and understanding

1. As a general rule, governments in 1700 did not take responsibility for the economy and transport as modern governments do. There are three exceptions in Units 1A to 1D. Which are they?

2. Most of the words in this list have changed their meaning since around 1700 or have fallen out of use altogether. Explain what people of around 1700 would have meant by the following:

    Navigation
    Manufacturing
    Port
    Sea coal
    Highway
    Parish
    Post-house
    Holloway
    Causeway

3. Give three statements or sources from 1A to 1D which support each of these statements:
    a) The most common private travellers on the roads were men travelling alone;
    b) An eighteenth century person was just as likely to think of a port as a place on a river as on the coast;
    c) All the sources of power used for transport in 1700 were natural not man-made;
    d) The volume of manufacturing and food production in 1700 could not have been reached without the transport system of the time.

A final note before you read Part Two

It would be fine for students if history took place in chunks and everything changed every twenty-five years or so. But it doesn't. Things from different times exist side by side. This book is written on a word-processor which could not have existed ten years ago, in a house which is ninety years old, in a road which was a farmers track in the middle ages and was given its modern shape more than a hundred years ago.

So history is full of 'mostly's'. Around 1700, people mostly travelled (if they travelled at all) in the way described in Part One. Most of the changes described in Part Two happened after 1700. But, as you will see, some of them began before then. In the same way, most of the forms of travel described in Part Two had disappeared by 1800, but you can find examples of pack-horses or barges on rivers into the twentieth century.

2

1700–1760s:
THE AGE OF THE IMPROVERS

This page reminds you of the changes in manufacturing and trade that were going on in the eighteenth century before the coming of steam power and factories. More goods and more trading led to improved means of transport. The improvements in transport by water started first (and actually began in the 1660s) but road improvements gathered pace by the 1720s.

A   Improving navigation – opening more miles of river to trade
B   Turnpiking the roads – making roads more suitable for traffic
C   Turnpike roads and trade – the growth of the road carrying business
D   Skills section: drawing conclusions from maps

Some key people

1709	Darby and coke smelting
1712	Newcomen and the atmospheric engine
1731	Tull and horse hoeing
1733	Kay and the flying shuttle
1764	Crompton and the spinning jenny

From London by fastest coach, summer 1760

Norwich	23 hours
Bath	30 hours
Manchester	46 hours
Edinburgh	160 hours

Output

Coal

1700	2.0 million tons
1730	5.2 million tons
1775	8.8 million tons

Pig iron

1720–4	27,000 tons
1740–4	26,000 tons
1760–4	34,000 tons

Soap

1713	24.4 million lbs
1733	27.7 million lbs
1763	29.6 million lbs

Candles

1713	31.6 million lbs
1733	34.3 million lbs
1763	42.7 million lbs

Printed cloth

1713	2.03 million yards
1733	2.92 million yards
1763	5.89 million yards

Shipping tonnage

1702	323,000 tons
1751	421,000 tons
1771	577,000 tons

Cattle and sheep taken to Smithfield market

1732	76,000 cattle	515,000 sheep
1762	103,000 cattle	722,000 sheep

Population	1700	1750
London	550,000	657,000
Liverpool	6,000	22,000
Manchester	10,000	18,000
Birmingham	5–7,000	23,000
Bristol	20,000	50,000

Before you read on, use these tables to find examples of:

a) the need to improve transport for i) heavy manufactured goods, ii) light household goods, iii) people;
b) causes of likely damage to roads;
c) the need to improve transport facilities for exporters and importers.

A IMPROVING NAVIGATION

Petitioners and Parliament

Merchants and mine-owners preferred to send heavy and bulky goods by water because of the savings on cost. That explains why the first efforts to improve the country's transport system had been to make more rivers navigable for more of their length. We can trace the great spurt in improvements back before the eighteenth century, to the 1660s when there were about 655 miles of navigable river and the transport map looked like this:

A

This map was drawn by a twentieth-century historian using many local records and travellers' accounts to work out for how long rivers were navigable.

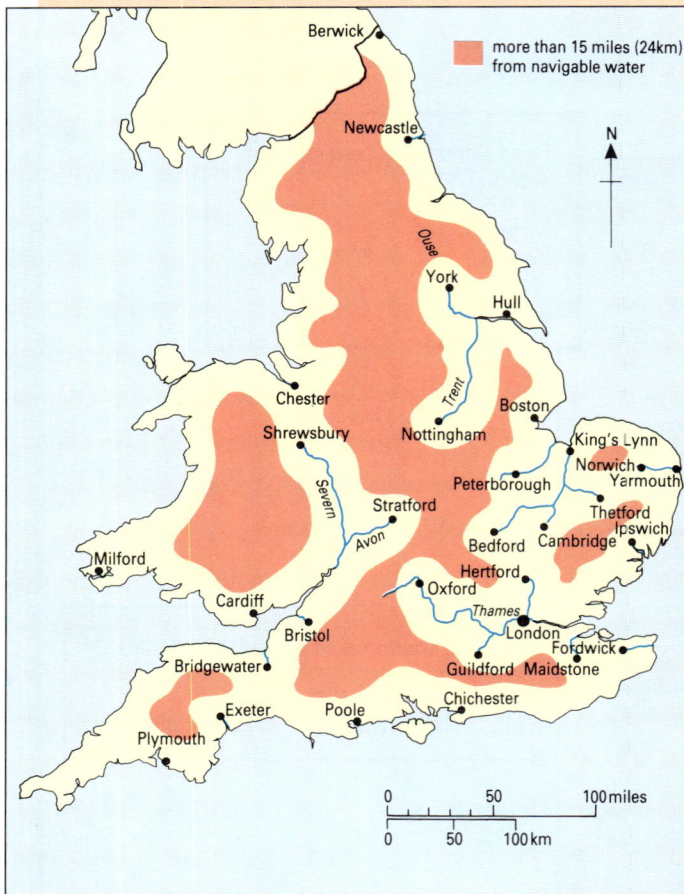

Map key: more than 15 miles (24km) from navigable water

Places marked: Berwick, Newcastle, York, Hull, Chester, Boston, Shrewsbury, Nottingham, King's Lynn, Norwich, Yarmouth, Peterborough, Stratford, Thetford, Ipswich, Milford, Avon, Bedford, Cambridge, Cardiff, Hertford, Oxford, Bristol, Thames, London, Fordwick, Bridgewater, Guildford, Maidstone, Exeter, Poole, Chichester, Plymouth. Rivers marked: Ouse, Trent, Severn.

Scale: 0 50 100 miles / 0 50 100 km

1. With the help of the map on page 1, list the products which it would be most difficult to get to market.

Fifteen miles was about as far as horses and men could haul carts, waggons and sledges in a day. Many manufacturers and merchants could cut their transport costs dramatically if they could be that close, or nearer, to navigable water. There was so much pressure for action that, between 1661 and 1665, MPs voted on twelve bills to improve stretches of river and passed them into law.

B

In 1665 the Speaker of the House of Commons explained the river laws.

> We have prepared some Bills for making small Rivers navigable; a Thing that in other Countries hath been more experienced, and hath been found very advantageous; it easeth the People of the great Charges of Land Carriages; preserves the Highways, which are daily worn out with Waggons carrying excessive Burdens; it breeds up a Nursery of Waterman which, upon Occasion, will prove good Seamen; and with much facility maintains Intercourse and Communion between Cities and Counties.

Journal of the House of Lords, 1675

2. The Speaker gave four advantages of river improvements. Can you list them?

The laws of the 1660s were quite different from Transport Acts of our day, which are usually prepared by the Department of Transport. In the 1660s there was no government department or minister of transport and no local authorities to carry out the work. The Bills had been asked for (or petitioned) by local merchants and landowners who wanted to improve transport in their district. Other people had petitioned Parliament not to pass them. Some opponents were owners of waggon or packhorse businesses. Others were farmers whose meadows went up the river-side or mill-owners who used the river water to turn their wheels. Yet Parliament usually agreed that the Bill was needed. After the twelve passed up to 1665, there were around another fifty by 1727. By then the 665 miles had grown to 1,160 and the river system looked like the map, source C.

Undertakers and engineers

Each of the Acts gave a group of 'undertakers' the power to undertake the improvement of the river. The undertakers were usually the people who had petitioned for the law. They needed the powers to force other people to accept change. They often had to compel landowners to have part of their land used as a towpath for men or horses pulling barges. They had to deal with the people who owned fishing rights or had mills on the river bank. A town corporation might have to be made to agree to bridges being raised. The whole undertaking would cost a lot of money, but the undertakers would get this back because the law gave them power to charge a toll on boats using their stretch of water.

The undertakers usually turned themselves into a company which would then pay an engineer to take charge of the work. His first task would be to improve the flow of the river. To keep the water running straight

C

The same historian brought the map on page 12 up to 1727 by checking Daniel Defoe's travel book to see how far river navigations went.

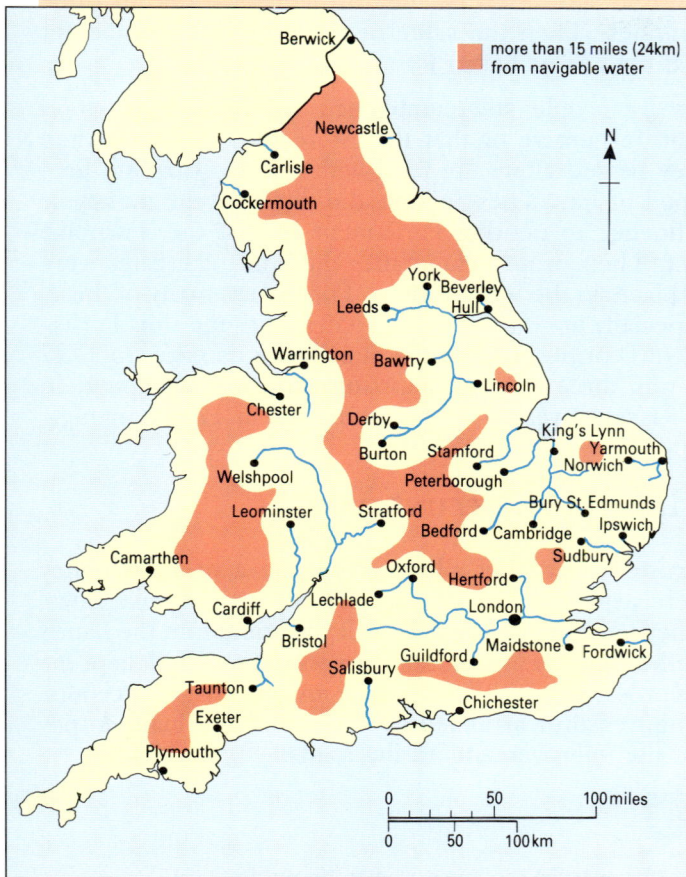

Map legend: more than 15 miles (24km) from navigable water

Towns shown: Berwick, Newcastle, Carlisle, Cockermouth, York, Beverley, Hull, Leeds, Warrington, Bawtry, Lincoln, Chester, Derby, King's Lynn, Burton, Stamford, Yarmouth, Norwich, Welshpool, Peterborough, Leominster, Stratford, Bury St Edmunds, Ipswich, Camarthen, Bedford, Cambridge, Sudbury, Oxford, Hertford, Cardiff, Lechlade, London, Bristol, Salisbury, Guildford, Maidstone, Fordwick, Taunton, Chichester, Exeter, Plymouth

Scale: 0 50 100 miles / 0 50 100 km

N

3. List rivers which had been made navigable and towns which had become inland ports since 1660.
4. What effect would the changes have on sales of
   a) iron products from the Midlands,
   b) stockings from Derbyshire,
   c) corn from Lincolnshire and East Anglia,
   d) cloth from Yorkshire,
   e) coal from the Wales-England borders?

and deep, bends had to be straightened, if possible, and the banks had to be firmed up. Willows were often planted on the banks to hold the earth with their roots and to stop boats coming too close.

Man-made obstacles were more difficult. The most common were weirs across the river to build up a supply of water. Most were placed there by mill-owners who ran the water through a passage which held their water-wheel. It then passed into the river further down stream leaving shallow water below the weir. In some cases the only way to move goods was to put them onto 'lightening boats' until the barge was light enough to be floated over the weir. The other way was to put paddles over the weir so that the water was stored behind them. This was a flash-lock. When the paddles were lifted a flood of water passed through and a convoy of barges could be floated over the rocks.

D

A nineteenth-century drawing showing paddles being lifted on a flash-lock on the Thames.

In some places engineers used a pound-lock instead of the flash. The pound-lock was the same as those in canals today. One or two barges were held between the walls of a narrow pound which had a gate at each end. When one of the gates was opened the water rose or fell to the level needed to go up or down stream. Pound-locks were expensive to build and could move far fewer boats at a time than the flash-lock.

E

One river improvement was an important pointer to the future. In 1697 Celia Fiennes was at Exeter:

> ...the River Ex which runs to Topshum [*Topham*] where the shipps come up to the barre; this is 7 miles by water which they are attempting to make navigable to the town which will be of mighty advantage to have ships come up close to the town to take in their serges, which they are now forced to send to Topsham on horses.

Celia Fiennes, *My Great Journey*, 1698

5. How is this a good illustration of how keen manufacturers were to improve waterways?

The Exe ran into Exeter, but after Topham the land rose so steeply that the water was too rough and shallow for ships. In 1699 work started on making a canal with pound-locks to bypass the unusable parts of the Exe. As Celia Fiennes shows, the great cost seemed worth it to local manufacturers even though they were cutting out only seven miles by packhorse.

Deadwater canals which did not use the flowing water of a river were common in Europe. The Exeter canal was the first successful one in Britain and showed engineers how the pound-lock could be used to carry water uphill. Yet no-one built another canal until 1755, when Parliament passed an Act to improve the tiny Sankey Brook which ran from the Mersey to St Helens. When it was finished in 1761 there was still no canal which ran between rivers or across country.

Justice Trusts

Between the 1660s and 1705, Parliament passed forty Acts to improve rivers and only seven which dealt with roads. The two kinds of Acts were different. River navigation was handed over to undertakers who formed private companies to raise the money needed. The laws for roads simply gave Justices of the Peace (JPs) extra powers to deal with the parishes whose roads were in a particularly bad state.

JPs had often said that it unfair to fine parishes who could not cope with the damage done by through traffic. So the Acts gave them powers to have toll-gates set up across the roads. In most cases it was not a gate but a long bar, pole or 'pike' which was turned after a toll was paid. The JPs used the money to have extra repair work done on the roads. In the meantime the people of the parish still had to give their labour free.

Turnpike trusts

The Acts applied to less than 100 miles of road and did little to improve things. Then, in 1706, a group of local people petitioned Parliament to give *them* the power to improve a length of road north of London and MPs passed the first Turnpike Act. The petitioners became the road's trustees and the Act said they could collect tolls to pay for road repair. This was the first turnpike trust. By 1760 there were more than 250. By the 1830s there were 1,116 in England and Wales.

A

Petitions for a Turnpike Act often began like this one of 1726 from 'several Gentlemen, Merchants, Tradesmen and other inhabitants living in and near the Road from Liverpool to Prescott.'

That the Road is very much used in the carriage of coals (to Liverpool and also from Liverpool) to the towns of Wigan, Bolton, Rochdale, Warrington and Manchester and to the counties of York, Derby and other eastern parts of the kingdom in the carriage of wool, cotton, malt and all their merchants goods; whereas several parts of the said road are so very deep, and other parts so narrow, that coaches, waggons and other wheeled vehicles cannot pass through the same; nor can the same be effectively repaired and enlarged, without some further provision be made for that purpose.

1. How was the road important?
2. What 'further provision' did the petioners mean?

For most Turnpike Acts there were objections from drovers, packhorsemen and waggon owners who protested that the road did not need repairs and that the tolls would put up costs. At first MPs took these objections so seriously that they turned down one in three petitions. Then the value of turnpikes became clearer and road users began to object less.

Poorer people still complained that tolls made food more expensive or that they were forced to pay when they passed along the road with a horse carrying firewood or hay. These people did not have the money or influence to petition Parliament against the Turnpike Act. Their protest came after the Turnpike gates were in place, in the form of riots. There were many of these, especially up to the 1750s. To deal with the riots Parliament kept pushing up the penalty for damage. In 1727 it was three months imprisonment and whipping, in 1731 seven years transportation and in 1734 hanging.

Making the trust work

Trustees were not allowed to make a profit but they were expected to run the trust on business-like lines. They usually put the day-to-day running into the hands of the clerk, treasurer, and surveyor. The Clerk kept the records and saw to advertisements for toll-gate keepers. The treasurer arranged subscriptions and loans to pay for the improvements to the roads.

B

A turnpike trust is going to be made from Cambridge to Ely for which purpose the subscriptions are begun with great encouragement, one for free gifts and the other for money to be lent on the credit of the tolls to be established by Act of Parliament on the said Turnpike road. The whole expense...will amount to £4,000 or upwards. The Lord Bishop, gentry and clergy of Ely have subscribed above £1,300, Lord Royston £500, and the late Mr Riste by will £200 and many other sums are promised.

Ipswich Journal, 24 December 1762

3. Which two kinds of subscription are asked for.
4. Roughly what proportion of the cost of making the road had been subscribed?
5. What reasons might the subscribers have in giving the money?

Turnpike trusts limited themselves to improving the surface of old highways. All surveyors agreed that the main problem was drainage. Water which settled on the road caused a quagmire. If it ran off in a stream it took the surface with it. The first step was always to have ditches dug at the sides of the road, but when it came to running the water into the drains there were nearly as many methods as there were surveyors. Some surveyors told workmen to make a curve from the centre. Some

D

A painting of a toll gate on a turnpiked road in the late eighteenth century.

7. Compare this with the picture of an unturnpiked road in Unit 1C. How strong is the evidence that turnpiking improved roads?

had the road cambered from one side to another. Others curved the materials inwards to make a gully down the centre while still others had 'grips' or channels across the road. None of the surfaces was fixed with tar so that filling-in repairs were always needed.

C

A decision by the Trustees of the Droitwich to Bromsgrove Turnpike, 1766.

Ordered that the surveyor do give notice to every person intending to take soil for manure or any other purpose from the side of the road that they must not take away the same as it is in general wanted for filling up the holloways.

6. What evidence does this provide about the science of roadwork?

General Wade and John Metcalfe

In the first half of the eighteenth century the only road-maker to earn a reputation was an army man. General Wade was in charge of making military roads in the Scottish Highlands at a time when many clans supported the Stuart family who had been turned off the throne in 1688. Their rebellious mood led to two rebellions in 1715 and 1745. Under his command, 250 miles were built up to 1840, and another 800 were completed by the man who took over from him. Their roads were four to five metres wide, built up in stages starting with large boulders, then stones and finally gravel. The idea of building a proper foundation was new, and so was road-making on such a scale – but then Wade could use soldiers as workers.

In the later eighteenth century a Yorkshire man built 180 miles of new roads for turnpike trusts in his county. John Metcalfe was the owner of a packhorse and waggon carrying business. 'Blind Jack' had lost his sight from smallpox as a child but he had an uncanny skill in leading his horses and waggons over difficult country-side. That helped him to understand the importance of good foundations. Wherever the ground was wet or soft, he began by having bundles of heather laid. He followed with a foundation of jagged stones fitted together before finishing with smaller stones and gravel, arranged to give the road a camber to drain off the water.

The turnpike network

Most turnpike trusts covered short lengths of road from two or three miles up to about twenty. Usually, when a district had its first trust, others quickly followed. In this way, all the main roads from London were turnpiked through most of their length by 1750. There were eighteen trusts on the Great North Road.

In the second half of the century the network of main roads was filled out with other roads which were important locally. Some benefited local mining and manufacturing, and many turnpikes were set up to provide roads for farm produce after villages were enclosed.

E

Milestones on the Ashbourne–Buxton turnpike in Derbyshire.

1738

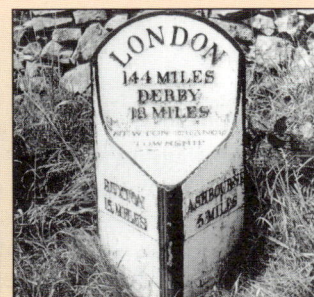

1777

8. Why were early mileposts made of stone and many later ones of cast-iron?

15

C TURNPIKE ROADS AND TRADE

In 1767 a writer commented on the importance of turn-pikes to goods transport.

A

There never was a more astonishing revolution, accomplished in the internal system of any country. The carriage of grain, coals, merchandise, etc is in general conducted with little more than half the number of horses which it formerly was . . . The hinge which has guided all these movements, and upon which they turn, is the reformation which has been made in our public roads.

Henry Homer, *Enquiry into the means of Preserving and Improving the Publick Roads*, 1767

1. What did Henry Homer mean by 'internal system'?
2. How does he account for the cheapening of road transport?

B   The carrying business

B1   An advertisement.

George Paschall, now the old Derby carrier to London, sends a Wagon from his House adjoining the Red-Lyon Inn in Derby every Monday and is at the Bull and Mouth Inn near Aldersgate, London every Saturday: Also sets out again every Monday from thence and is at his house every Friday or Saturday following. Note, That those are the days of setting out and coming in, for the Winter season and all Persons that are disposed to travel by the said Waggon shall have Handsome Usage; also those that have Goods or Parcels of any kind to send or have brought shall be kindly received and well used: He also returns money to and from London but if any be put into parcels unknown to him or without Notice given to his Bookeepers thereof, he will not be accountable for any such money lost.

Derby Mercury, 27 December 1733

3. In what sense was George Paschall running a 'stage' waggon service?
4. List the services he was offering.
5. How might his summer service have been different?
6. What do you learn about the importance of inns to the carriers from sources B1 and B3?
7. Make notes to B2 to show how it is useful as evidence about road conditions, regulations for vehicles, traffic on the roads and the freight carried.
8. Which services advertised in B1 are shown in B3?

The carriers

Behind the improvements noted by Henry Homer was a boom in business for carriers. A carrier was the owner of a fleet of waggons each pulled by six or eight horses. Even the small improvements of the worst turnpike trusts were enough to make it possible to send them at a steady speed of two or three miles per hour. In many towns the leading carriers began stage-waggon services which worked to a timetable for each stage of the journey. The staging posts were inns where goods were delivered to be loaded or could be off-loaded to wait for a connection going in a different direction. Stage-waggons often carried a passenger or two as well.

B2   A waggon on the road.

B3   A late eighteenth century drawing of passengers boarding a waggon after having spent the night in a country inn.

16

B4 An eighteenth-century survey of the changes.

the chapmen used to keep gangs of packhorses, and accompany them to the principal towns with goods in packs... On the improvement of turnpike roads waggons were set up, and the packhorses discontinued; and the chapmen only rode out for orders, carrying with them patterns in their bags. It was during the forty years from 1730 to 1770 that trade was greatly pushed by the practice of sending these riders all over the kingdom.

John Aikin, *A Description of the Country from Thirty to Forty Miles around Manchester*, 1798

9. In your own words, explain the changes described by John Aikin.

Stage-waggons took little trade away from the rivers which were still much cheaper for bulky goods but they were a more serious threat to packhorse businesses. Some carriers such as Pickfords changed from running packhorse teams to waggons. Merchants often gave up sending goods by packhorses to villages and towns to sell as they went along. Instead they employed 'riders', which was the common name for travelling salesmen. They went out with a book of samples to take orders which were then delivered by waggon.

Road users v road makers

Waggons and their horses did great damage to road surfaces so the turnpike trusts were keen supporters of the laws passed to limit this. The first laws tried to control the weight of waggons and the number of horses pulling them. Later Acts laid down widths for the felly, or rim, of the wheel. From 1753 waggons on turnpike roads had to have fellies of nine inches (22.8 cm) or more. In 1757 trusts were ordered to charge such waggons only a half-toll while narrow wheeled waggons had to pay 1½ tolls. In 1765 the half-toll was only legal if the front and back parts of wheels were different lengths apart so that the waggon rolled a sixteen-inch (40 cm) path. In 1773 all the regulations about weight, width and number of horses were drawn together in one General Turnpike Act.

Private travel

Up to the 1760s or 1770s stage-coach services for passenger traffic developed less quickly than the waggon trade. The turnpike roads still did not give a fast and comfortable ride. The coaches themselves were cramped and badly sprung so that to be 'coached' came to mean suffering from a nasty kind of travel sickness.

Private road transport probably changed faster, especially around towns. Most towns had turnpike roads running into the countryside like the spokes on a wheel –

and today you can often see eighteenth-century houses built by men who could travel to their town-centre businesses from them.

C

Turnpikes around London, described in 1798.

The turnpike roads in Middlesex bear evident marks of their vicinity to a great city. Scattered villas and genteel houses... are erected on one or both sides of the roads, for three, five or seven miles out of London. The foot-paths are thronged with passengers, and the carriage-ways with horses, carts, waggons, chaises and gentlemen's carriages of every description.

J. Middleton, *View of the Agriculture of Middlesex*, 1798

10. Why should the well-to-do have moved out of town?
11. Which two forms of transport did they use?

As John Middleton tells us, 'Gentlemen', were beginning to find it worthwhile to buy carriages for their family use. Generally these were still not used over long distances. Men often rode on horseback or took up the new fashion of travelling by chaise, a light carriage for one or two people pulled by one or two horses. You could travel "post' by chaise which meant that you changed the horses at post-inns every few miles. Chaises were certainly a sign of road improvement. In 1698 Celia Fiennes could have made her journey only on horseback. In 1768 and 1770 Arthur Young travelled through most of Britain using a chaise. As you might expect, he found great differences in the quality of turnpike roads.

D

Two turnpike roads described by Arthur Young.

... that from Salisbury, to four miles the other side of Romsey... It is everywhere broad enough for 3 carriages to pass each other; and lying in straight lines, with an even edge of grass the whole way, it has more the appearance of an elegant gravel walk, than of a high-road.

A Young, *Southern Tour*, 1768

To Newcastle Turnpike. This, in general, is a paved causeway, as narrow as can be conceived and cut into perpetual holes, some of them two feet deep... I was forced to hire two men at one place to support my chaise from overthrowing, in turning out for a cart of goods overthrown and almost buried...

A Young, *Northern Tour*, 1770

12. Suggest reasons for the difference between these two roads.

D SKILLS SECTION

Drawing conclusions from maps

A

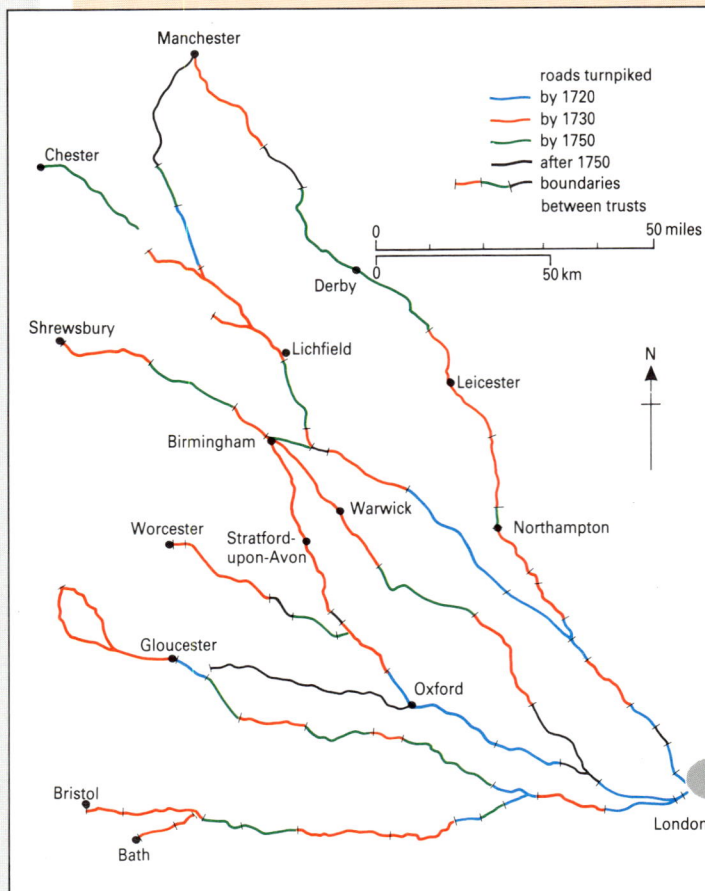

A1   Turnpike roads from London to the north-west.

Legend:
roads turnpiked
- by 1720
- by 1730
- by 1750
- after 1750
- boundaries between trusts

Places on A1: Manchester, Chester, Derby, Shrewsbury, Lichfield, Leicester, Birmingham, Warwick, Northampton, Worcester, Stratford-upon-Avon, Gloucester, Oxford, Bristol, Bath, London

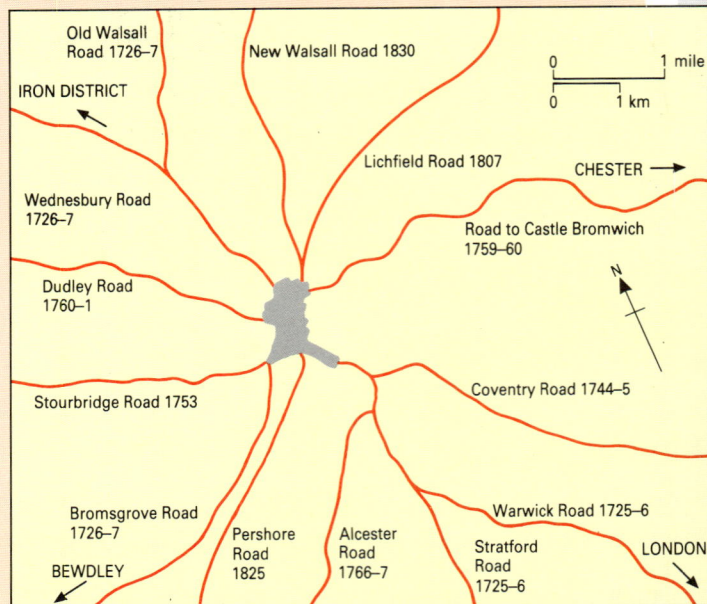

A2   Turnpike roads around Birmingham.

Labels on A2: Old Walsall Road 1726–7, New Walsall Road 1830, IRON DISTRICT, Wednesbury Road 1726–7, Lichfield Road 1807, CHESTER, Dudley Road 1760–1, Road to Castle Bromwich 1759–60, Stourbridge Road 1753, Coventry Road 1744–5, Bromsgrove Road 1726–7, Pershore Road 1825, Alcester Road 1766–7, Warwick Road 1725–6, Stratford Road 1725–6, BEWDLEY, LONDON

1. Which sections of the roads to London were the first to be turnpiked? Why was this?
2. Suggest two reasons for the first turnpikes in Birmingham.
3. Give two examples of ways in which the maps support each other.

Knowledge and understanding

1. Make a chart listing the similarities and differences between turnpike trusts and navigation companies using these headings:

   Reasons for being set up
   Methods of working
   Effects on travel
   Effects on goods carriage

2. From the information in this Part, including page 11, make a list of reasons for the improvements in transport during these years.

3. How would you account for the fact that by 1761 Britain had only two very short lengths of deadwater canal while the continent had many miles?

3

1760s – c.1830: TRANSPORT AND THE EARLY INDUSTRIAL REVOLUTION

Coal, iron and textiles were at the centre of the industrial revolution but it also involved other industries such as pottery and chemicals. Most of the changes could not have taken place without the canals for moving the many extra thousand tonnes of coal, iron, bales of cotton or crates of chinaware. Towns could not have grown without the bargeloads of flour and sugar which came in to feed their people. Just as necessary to factory owners and merchants, were the great improvements in the speed by which people and mail could move along the roads.

A Bridgewater and Brindley – the early canals
B Developing the canal system
C Travel and transport by canal
D Road builders – the work of Telford and McAdam
E The coaching revolution – faster journey times for people and mail
F Skills section: interpreting pictures

Main areas of industrialisation by c.1830

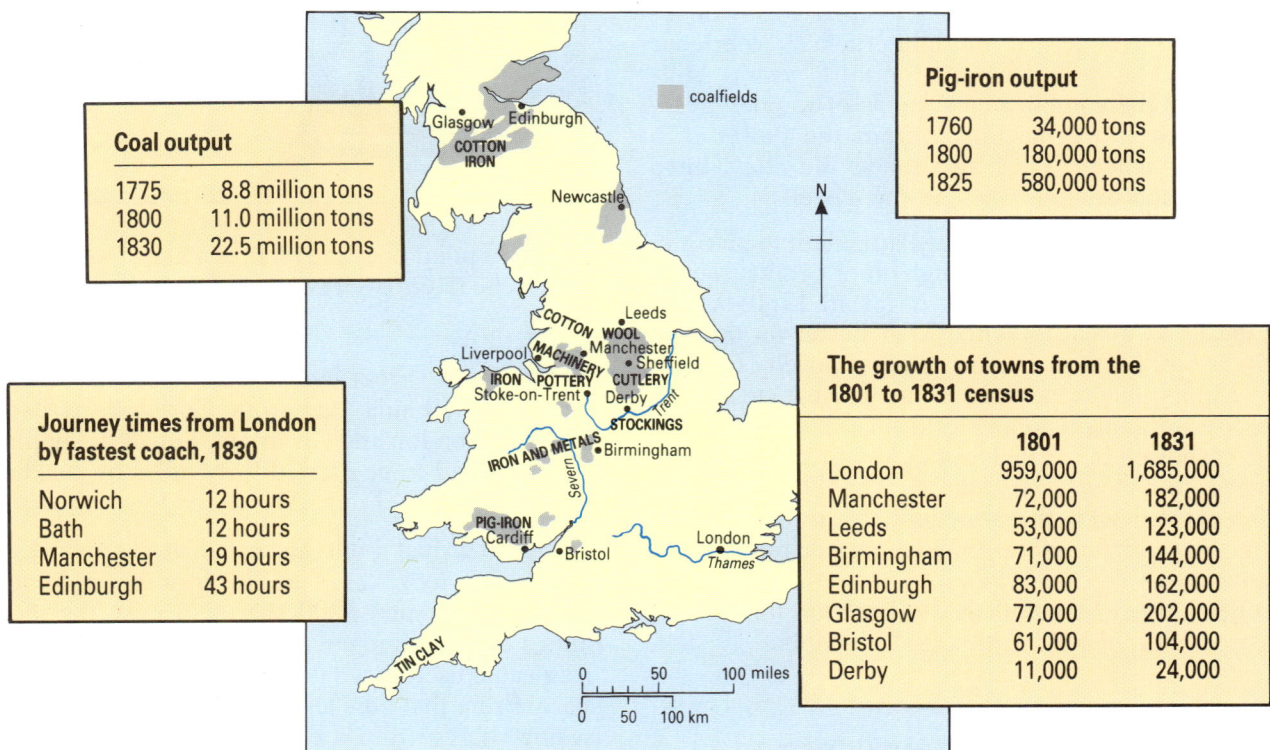

Coal output

1775	8.8 million tons
1800	11.0 million tons
1830	22.5 million tons

Pig-iron output

1760	34,000 tons
1800	180,000 tons
1825	580,000 tons

Journey times from London by fastest coach, 1830

Norwich	12 hours
Bath	12 hours
Manchester	19 hours
Edinburgh	43 hours

The growth of towns from the 1801 to 1831 census

	1801	1831
London	959,000	1,685,000
Manchester	72,000	182,000
Leeds	53,000	123,000
Birmingham	71,000	144,000
Edinburgh	83,000	162,000
Glasgow	77,000	202,000
Bristol	61,000	104,000
Derby	11,000	24,000

Before you read on, can you think of:

a) two ways in which deadwater canals were an improvement on rivers for moving goods between centres of industry or to ports;

b) three advantages a textile manufacturer in Manchester would see in being able to visit London (or send a letter) in about twenty-four hours on every day of the week rather than in about forty-eight hours on some days of the week.

In 1748 the second Duke of Bridgewater died. His twelve-year-old son, Francis, became duke and owner of the family estates at Worsley, north-west of Manchester. There was coal under the Worsley land and the Duke's agent managed the mines. The profits paid for the third Duke to finish his education with a Grand Tour of Europe, looking at the art collections, the European ladies of his own class and some of France's many long canals.

In 1757 he came home and was soon listening to his agent's plans for the mines. Seven miles away there was the growing textile town of Manchester. Its people needed coal to heat their homes and for their manufacturing. Even before steam engines, large quantities were used for heating to make beer, candles, glass and, above all, to wash and dye cloth.

The Worsley coal was carried to the Irwell, a river which had been made navigable by the Mersey and Irwell Company. But it was a long struggle for halers to pull barges to Manchester. Bridgewater's agent suggested they build a canal and that James Brindley would be the man to do the work. Brindley was self-educated and it often showed. He wrote to the Duke that he had done an 'ochilor servey or ricconitoring' (ocular survey or reconnoitering). But he had the right practical experience after working as a mill-wright for thirty years. Millwrights built the complicated systems of wooden gear-wheels which drove machinery from the power of a single water wheel. They also made the stone-lined channels which brought water to the wheel.

The Duke first needed an Act of Parliament to give him the power to cut the canal through other people's lands. The Act was passed and work began in 1760. A year later the Duke's coals reached Manchester on the first cross-country canal in Britain. Such a novelty brought many visitors, magazine writers and artists. Most came to see the aqueduct which Brindley had built across the Irwell. It showed how canals could free themselves from the need to follow river valleys. The Duke had his picture painted with the aqueduct in the background (Source A), and the picture made another point about the advantages of canals. The point was driven home when he charged Mancunians 3½d per ton for his coal compared with 7d before the canal was open.

Brindley and the silver cross

The Bridgewater Canal started a new era in transport history. The Duke and Brindley were first off the mark with a new Act of Parliament to extend their canal from Manchester to the Mersey near Liverpool. The work was finished by 1767. By then a group of manufacturers in the midlands had seen the possibility of linking their district with the main rivers and ports on both sides of the country. The most enthusiastic was Josiah Wedgwood who was building up his chinaware business in the

A

1. What point does the picture make about transport on the river Irwell compared with on the canal?

towns around Stoke-on-Trent. The firm used large quantities of china clay from Cornwall. It had sales offices in London and Liverpool. Yet all its supplies and deliveries had to be carried forty miles by packhorse to one of the rivers Trent, Mersey or Severn.

Bridgewater had built his canal at his own expense. Wedgwood took the lead in forming a joint stock company. It issued £200 shares to raise the money to build a canal. When the company began to make income from canal users it would pay a yearly dividend on each share. From that time all canals were built by companies issuing shares.

In 1766, after Parliament had passed an Act, the Company started work on the Trent & Mersey Canal. In the planning stage it had been called the Grand Trunk because of the number of branches it would have. Two of the most important links had been decided already. Wedgwood and Bridgewater agreed that their canals should meet so that they could use one set of locks into the Mersey and so boats on the Trent & Mersey could reach Manchester. The second link would be into the River Severn via the Staffordshire &

Worcestershire Canal. The Act for this was passed on the same day as the one for the Trent & Mersey.

James Brindley played a leading part in planning the routes and building all these canals. He was already talking about a 'silver cross' which would link the four great rivers of England. The Trent & Mersey would provide two arms and the third would come with the Staffordshire and Worcestershire. Brindley had planned this to join the Severn at the busy inland port of Bewdley which was crowded with packhorses and waggons moving goods between the river and the manufacturing centres of the midlands. The people of Bewdley decided they did not want his 'stinking ditch' so Brindley took it a few miles south to Stourport, where there was just one house. Stourport grew into a flourishing town and Bewdley became a quiet backwater. In 1768 and 1769 Parliament passed Acts for the Coventry and Oxford Canals which would make the fourth arm linking the Trent & Mersey with the River Thames.

The narrow canals

The canals made by Brindley and the engineers who worked with him were built when there were few skilled canal workers, no steam power for driving machinery and no iron tracks for running carts and equipment to and from the diggings. As far as possible Brindley followed the contours of the land to cut down the number of embankments, cuttings and locks needed to cope with different levels. Yet, they could not always be avoided. For instance, the Trent & Mersey had to cross the southern Pennines and to do this Brindley built the country's first transport tunnel, 2,408 metres long, at Harecastle. He built the canals to take seven-feet-wide (2.1 m) 'narrow boats' like those on the Bridgewater canals. Narrowness cut the building costs of the canals and their bridges, as well as any locks and embankments or tunnels which could not be avoided.

The major canals encouraged other companies to build shorter links, especially around Birmingham where Brindley again played a leading part. The Birmingham Canal ran into the town from the Staffordshire & Worcestershire, so it linked the city with Liverpool and Bristol and also brought Staffordshire coal cheaply into Birmingham. The Birmingham & Fazely Canal linked in with the Coventry Canal and on to the Thames.

All these schemes were started by 1772, the year when Brindley died from a chill which overwork made fatal. They were not all completed until 1789, but Brindley's work from 1761 to 1772, when he planned the silver cross to open midlands coal, iron and pottery to the rest of England and the world, was one of the most important stages in industrial history.

Brindley had also started other people thinking about cross country routes. The Severn & Thames Canal was being dug as another link between England's great rivers. Parliament had passed an Act for the Leeds & Liverpool Canal across the Pennines, which Brindley had also surveyed. In Scotland work had started on the Forth & Clyde Canal to link the east and west coasts.

B

B1   Map of canals in 1789.

B2   The last section of the Trent and Mersey was opened in July 1777. A Stoke-on-Trent carrying company, Hugh Henshall & Co, advertised some of its charges per ton and compared them with land transport. The Staffordshire & Worcestershire and the Birmingham Canal were already open.

Between	Canal			Land		
	£	s	d	£	s	d
Manchester and Etruria		15	0	2	15	0
Manchester and Nottingham	2	0	0	4	0	0
Manchester and Birmingham	1	10	0	4	0	0
Manchester and Stourport	1	10	0	4	13	4
Liverpool and Etruria		13	4	2	10	0
Liverpool and Birmingham	1	10	0	5	0	0
Gainsboro' and Birmingham	1	10	0		–	

From: *Aris's Birmingham Gazette*, 21 July 1777

2. With the help of the text name each of canals 1 to 9.
3. Explain what Brindley meant by the 'silver cross' and where it lies on the map. How much was completed by 1777?
4. Compare this map with Map B in Unit 2A (page 12). What does the comparison show about the importance of Brindley's work?

B DEVELOPING THE CANAL SYSTEM

Mania in the 1790s

The first canals were seen as a great success, especially for people earning good dividends on their shares. A person who had bought a £100 share in the Birmingham Canal Company in 1767 received £23 as dividend in 1789. Some companies had done less well but these did not attract so much attention. Shareholders' profits made canal companies different from turnpike trusts which did not pay dividends and from the Navigation Companies who were often heavily in debt.

The chance of profits was one of the forces which led to a canal-building boom in the 1790s. It has sometimes been called the 'canal mania' because of the way that people rushed to put money into companies. Parliament passed fifty-two Acts for new canals between 1790 and 1796, twenty of them in 1793 which was the peak year.

The canal mania was not only about money-making. It was an important sign of how Britain was changing from being a manufacturing to an industrial country. Boulton and Watt's steam engine was on sale from 1775. Henry Cort invented puddling and rolling of iron in 1784. Spinning mills were going up all over Derbyshire, Lancashire and Lanarkshire. Just as companies today put their new buildings near motorways, so the new factories and warehouses of the 1790s were built near canals.

The canal engineers could make use of the new products. The first ever iron bridge was built over the River Severn in 1769 and there were several ironworks who could supply the parts for short iron bridges over canals, or iron troughs to hold water in aqueducts. Coalmines and ironworks used iron rails for tramways to run their horse-drawn carts on. Canal companies often built tramroads to their canals, especially in South Wales. Steam engines were used to wind miners and coal up pit-shafts and it was not long before they were hauling loaded tubboats up a ramp or 'inclined plane'. The longest of these lifted boats from the Coalbrookdale works on the River Severn to the Shropshire canal, seventy metres above.

The wide canals

The new canals often cost more than the companies had expected. One reason was that the engineers were much more daring than Brindley. They built wide canals which could take boats much broader than seven feet (2.1 m) with loads of up to fifty tonnes instead of twenty. They also took more direct routes instead of following the contours. This meant extra work on making embankments over low ground and cuttings or tunnels through the steeper places, which added enormously to the cost. The most important of the new wide canals was the Grand Junction which linked Birmingham with London. Its ninety-three miles were hardly any longer than the road route and they by-passed the narrow-boat way through Oxford.

Some of the most dramatic canals crossed the Pennines. This often meant flights of several locks together. The first canal finished was the Rochdale Canal with ninety-two locks and two very short tunnels in thirty-three miles. The Huddersfield Canal had a tunnel of 5,456 yards (5 km) and seventy-four locks in twenty miles.

Canals and rivers

After the 1760s hardly any more miles of river were improved. In some cases the navigation company lost all its business to canal rivals. In others the river companies improved their business by building canals to by-pass difficult stretches of river or to make new links into the river. The Aire & Calder Navigation Company in Yorkshire increased its profits greatly after it opened the Goole Canals.

A

Growth of the inland navigation system:

England and Wales

1760	1,398 miles	1810	3,456 miles
1770	1,617 miles	1820	3,691 miles
1780	2,091 miles	1830	3,875 miles
1790	2,229 miles	1840	4,003 miles
1800	3,074 miles	1850	4,023 miles

1. In which ten-year period was the greatest number of miles added?
2. Why were only a few miles added after 1830?

B

John Fulton was himself an engineer who made part of the Peak Forest Canal but he was better known as a writer. His book, *A Treatise on the Improvement of Canal Navigation*, showed tub-boats being lifted between canals. He had seen this system at work on Shropshire canals.

3. When would an incline plane be more suitable than locks?

C

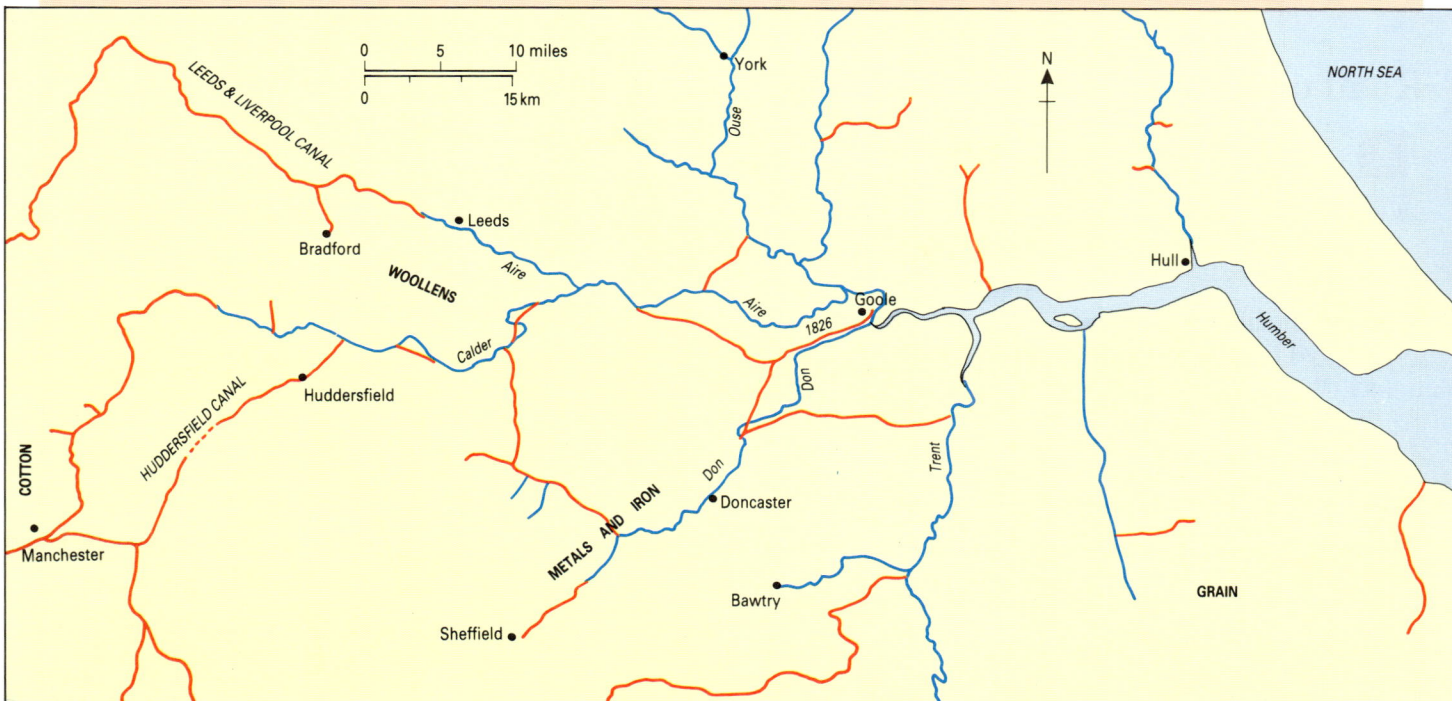

Navigable rivers and canals in Yorkshire c.1800.

4. How does this map help to explain why the Aire Calder River Navigation Company grew more profitable in the canal age?

5. Suggest a way of dividing the canals into three groups. Give each a title and name the canals you have chosen for the group.

6. How did the waterway system help each of the main products shown on the map?

D

In 1821 the population of Goole was 508. By 1841 it was 3,629. This report was written on the day that the canal links with the Don and Calder were opened.

A large and commodious inn, called the Banks Arms Hotel, is already opened and fitted up in capital style. On the north of it, is to be a spacious market place, 220 yards square. Several streets are staked out, in parallel lines, branching west fom the Ouse; some of these are 60 feet wide, with flagged causeways already laid . . . The houses in front of three or four of these streets are already built, and many of them occupied; when the whole now contracted for, are completed, they will amount to about 120. Those of the lowest class are finished in a style of neatness very unusual.

Hull Advertiser, 21 July 1826

7. What does the extract suggest about the connection between the canal and the growth of Goole's population?

8. How would the appearance of Goole in the 1830s differ from most towns of the same size?

E

Canals and tramroads of the valleys above Cardiff c.1815.

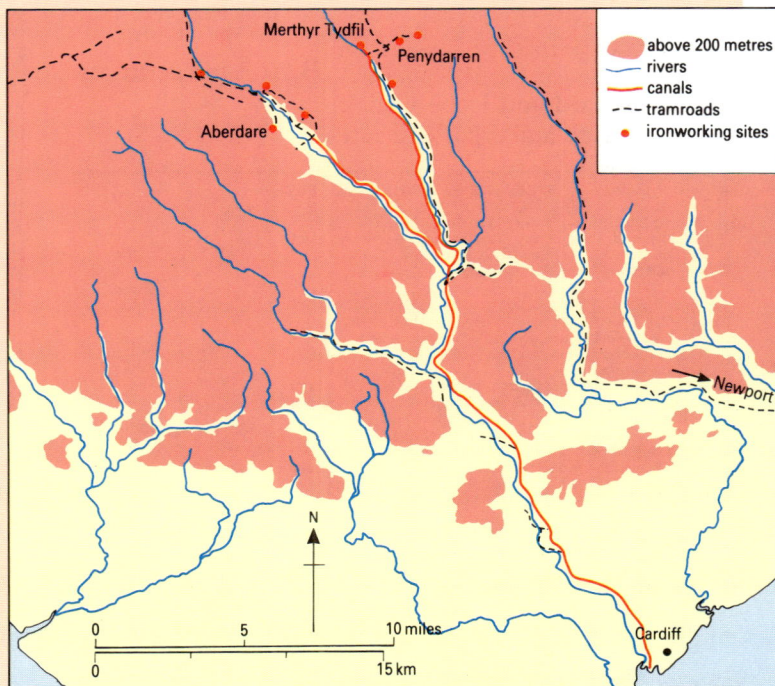

9. What proportion of the mileage was covered by water?

10. Why were so many tramroads built instead of canals?

23

Road or canal?

A

Lydia Sutton was the Liverpool agent for the London carrying firm of James Holt. In 1797 she wrote to him:

> The cannals now runs very quick – Mr R Hims wanted four piano Fortes down, two he ordered by canal, the other two by our wagon (as 2 of them were immediately wanted). Those by Canal arrived 3 days before those by our wagon . . . Canal delivered them the 9th day, ours the 12th. The difference in ye carriage was 10/– more by us than those by canal . . .
>
> The Irish Tea and Hop merchants tells me they wonder how we get any Business as they pay Pickford no more than 6/– p/cwt & I receive 9/6 – As for the Irish linens I do all that lays in my power to get more but it is impossible while the canal . . . under carry us.

In Waterways Museum, Stoke Bruerne

1. Lydia Sutton probably had a difficult time with Mr Hims! What complaints would he have been making?
2. What evidence is there that James Holt would be well advised to follow the example of Pickfords?
3. Use the map on page 21 to find the canal route used for the pianos.

B

B2	A toll certificate.

B1 Liskeard and Looe Canal: tonnage and wharfage rates.

TONNAGE AND WHARFAGE RATES.		
	s. d.	
For all Lime-stone, Culm or Coal for burning Lime, Sand, Oreweed, Dung or any other Manure, except Salt and Burnt Lime, Building-stone, Free-stone, Granite, Clay and Stone for making Roads	0 3½	per Ton, per Mile.
For Lime	0 7	ditto. ditto.
For all Wheat, Barley, Oats, Bran, Flour, Meal and Potatoes	0 10	ditto. ditto.
For all Tin-ore, Copper-ore, Lead-ore, Iron-stone, Antimony, Manganese, and all other Metals, Semi-Metals and Minerals not smelted, Coals and Culm not used for burning Lime	0 7	ditto. ditto.
For all Tin, Copper, Lead, Iron, and all other Metals having been smelted, Bricks, Tiles, Timber, Charcoal, Deals, Wood, Faggots, Bark, Seeds, Vetches, Peas, Paper, Old Junk or Rags, Salt and all other Goods, Wares, Merchandize and Things whatever, Hay, Straw, Cattle, Calves, Sheep, Swine and other Beasts	1 1½	ditto. ditto.
For all Goods, Wares, Merchandize and Things landed on any Wharf, but not remaining more than Seventy-two Hours	0 9	per Ton.
For ditto after the first Seventy-two Hours	0 6	ditto, per Day.
Fractions of a Ton to be taken as the Quarters therein, and of a Quarter as a Quarter. Fractions of a Mile as the Quarters, and of a Quarter as a Quarter.		

Joseph Priestley, *Historical Account of the Navigable Rivers, Canals and Railways of Great Britain*, 1831

4. Canal rates often favoured local farmers and local turnpike trusts. What evidence is there for that in this scale?

Income

Every stretch of canal had a clerk who made the charge and gave the steerer a ticket to show that payment had been made. The weight of the cargo could be seen by the gauge on the boat side which measured the depth it lay in the water.

Expenditure

The expenses of running the canal were huge. Instead of today's few pleasure craft in the summer months, a busy canal might have a hundred or more heavily laden barges passing through each day all year round. The wear and tear was so great that most locks had to be

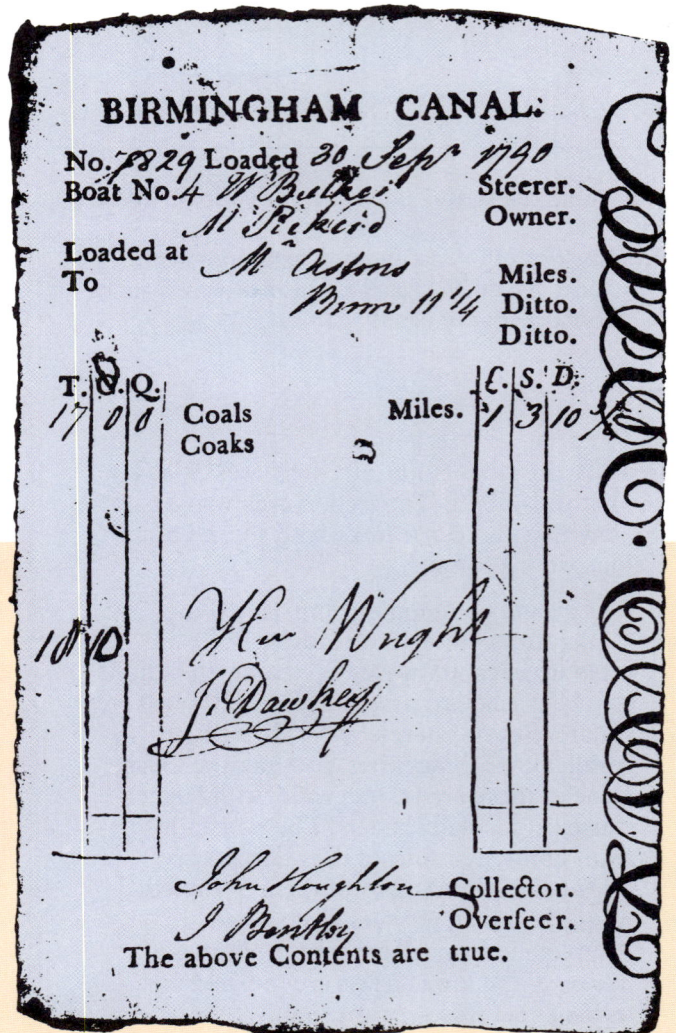

5. Are the different charges quite haphazard or can you see any reason for them? If so, what is it?
6. How could you use this scale to illustrate the importance of canals to industry and agriculture?
7. What is the purpose of the document in source B2?
8. The rate was about 1½d per ton per mile. Why might it have been cheaper than the rates in B1?

closed for repairs for a week or so each year. Keeping the canals open at other times meant using dredgers and ice-breakers. Every lock needed a keeper. He could easily bring a canal to a standstill by letting water drain through the gates or not using the locks economically. Wherever possible that meant waiting until there were two boats, not one, to enter the lock.

Canal carriers

Only a small number of canal boatmen were 'number ones' which meant that they owned their own boat. All the others worked for one of two kinds of fleets. The first kind were owned by mines, iron works and factories and were used only for their own products. The others belonged to carrying companies like those in the advertisements below. Often these had begun as land carriers before they moved over to canal.

Firms such as Skey, Small and Co owned barges carrying twenty tonnes on narrow canals and fifty on broad canals. They needed two people to work them, one to steer and the other to lead the single horse which pulled the barge from the towpath. At first this crew was usually a man and a boy. The early boatmen had their family home near the canal and the boats were built without cabins. If they were away from home they would take cheap lodgings in the canal-side inn.

By the early 1800s boats were being built with cabins which were the floating home of the boatmen and his family who would do the work of the second crew member. The change seems to have come partly because the time away from home grew longer as the number of miles of canal increased. Another reason was that canal companies kept wages low and boatmen found it difficult to afford the rent for their cottage.

Pickfords was the largest firm in the fly-boat business although there were many others. They had pioneered stage-waggons which left and arrived at fixed times. They did the same on the canals with their fly-boats. These carried only fifteen tonnes and used pairs of horses in relays and a crew of four, two working and two asleep. The fly-boats could average three miles per hour, day and night which meant they out-paced stage-waggons which could not travel by night.

Passenger boats developed from fly-boats. In a few places they became serious rivals to stage-coaches. Like them they carried parcels and packets but their main business was passengers. The journey was far smoother and passengers could be served with refreshments. In 1831 you could book a sleeping cabin for the fifty-five mile (89 km) journey from Glasgow to Edinburgh which took less than eleven hours. For the shorter journey from Paisley to Glasgow, which would be used by people going to work and shoppers, there were twelve ninety-passenger boats each way.

C

C1

A market-boat decked over with seats, and a fire place for the accommodation of passengers, starts from Swarkestone every Friday morning to carry market people to Derby, at 6d each; which again leaves Derby at 4 oclock for Swarkestone.

J. Farey, *General View of the Agriculture of Derbyshire*, 1817

C2

EXPEDITOUS WATER CONVEYANCE FROM BIRMINGHAM TO LEICESTER, &c

MESSRS PICKFORD beg leave to inform their Friends and the Public in General, that they have established a Pair of FLY STAGE BOATS weekly from hence to Leicester, and intermediate Places, which load goods at Birmingham every Thursday Afternoon, Warwick every Friday, Banbury and Oxford every Saturday; and discharge at Market Harborough and Leicester every Monday, return from Leicester every Monday evening; discharge Warwick Goods every Wednesday; and Birmingham every Thursday morning.

Aris's Birmingham Gazette, 28 November 1814

C3 A fly-boat night service for mixed goods. From the cover of a Clyde Canal Co brochure, 1835

C4

Skey, Small & Co's boats load at Birmingham and Wolverhampton 'every Spring Tides, three days before the Full and Change of Moon, for Bristol, Gloucester and all western parts of England.

Aris's Birmingham Gazette, 5 July 1813

9. Who would you expect to see on the Swarkestone–Derby boat?
10. Why did Skey, Small and Co link their journeys to the tides?
11. What do you think the words 'FLY' and 'STAGE' mean in the Pickfords advertisement?
12. Which form of transport was challenged by the Packet Boat service on the Clyde canal?
13. How would you describe each of the four kinds of service described here?

By the 1770s most main roads were turnpiked and the worst horrors for the traveller had disappeared. You were not likely to get drowned in a pothole or lost in the lanes. Carrier services were running to timetables. But improved roads bring more traffic, which wants to travel with greater speed and comfort, and a new round of complaints starts. This happens with motorways today and it happened with the turnpike roads when stage-coach services became more frequent from the 1750s. Road conditions held them down to four or five miles per hour. Coaches often broke-down from the jolting. Passengers were thrown about and had to dismount when gradients were too steep. Most coaches could manage only four inside- and four outside-passengers before they became dangerously over-loaded.

Travellers blamed the turnpike trusts. It was said they did not have enough money to spend. In 1762 the Cambridge to Ely turnpike road cost £4,000 compared with a quarter-of-a-million pounds for the Trent & Mersey Canal. Canal engineers used sub-contractors and large teams of workers. A turnpike trust engineer might have only a few dozen men. James Brindley had made more miles of canal than John Metcalfe had built roads. These differences were the background to the work of the two great road specialists of the early nineteenth century, Thomas Telford and John McAdam.

Telford

Thomas Telford was the son of a Scottish shepherd. He was apprenticed as a stone-mason which seems a humble start for the man who became Britain's greatest civil engineer. Yet a good mason could rise in the way that a mill-wright such as Brindley could. Telford added architecture to his skills and went to work in London, and then Portsmouth where he was in charge of building work at the docks. Then, still only thirty, he moved to Shropshire as the county surveyor in charge of the up-keep of buildings such as the jail and hospital as well as many bridges. Five years later he was combining this with being engineer to two canal companies.

Canal building proved that Telford was a skilled organiser. He could plan the work of different contractors so that earth removed from a cutting was used as an embankment a little further on. He saw the importance of labour saving devices such as iron plateways to run carts on. He pioneered a new use of iron when he used it to line the aqueduct which carried the water over the arches at Pontyscylte.

In 1802 his reputation brought him a new job. The government asked him to report on ways of developing the economy of Scotland to stop the flow of people moving to England or to Canada. Telford suggested twin schemes, one for the Caledonian Canal and the other for a big programme of road building. In 1803 the government put him in charge of both.

By 1816 he had been responsible for 920 miles of roads with 1,117 bridges. For each few miles of road and each bridge he used different contractors. Telford was working on a scale which no road engineer had ever reached and in thirteen years in Scotland he built more miles of road than Brindley built canals in eleven.

While he was still in charge of work in Scotland, Telford was given another government project, to complete a complaint-free road from London to Holyhead. The entire length had been turnpiked from 1805 but the surface was often bad while the gradients were too steep and the curves too sharp for fast stage coaches. This led to hold-ups – and a string of complaints from MPs. In 1801 Ireland had been united with England and MPs from Ireland now travelled across the Irish sea and then from Holyhead to London. Services used by politicans often get improved faster than those used by the general public, and in 1815 Parliament set up a Holyhead Road Commission with Telford as its engineer to build a fast coaching road to London.

In fifteen years he built the best coaching road in the country. As far as Shrewsbury, he made the turnpike trusts accept his higher standards in return for being able to charge higher tolls. From Shrewbury onwards the turnpike trusts were amalgamated into a single trust which was managed by Telford. His attention to detail could be seen right through this stretch. The bridges, mile-posts and toll-houses were graceful and so was his suspension bridge over the Menai Straits. When the road (which we call the A5) was finished, the mail coach from London reached Holyhead in under twenty-seven hours; before Telford started his work, the journey took forty-two hours.

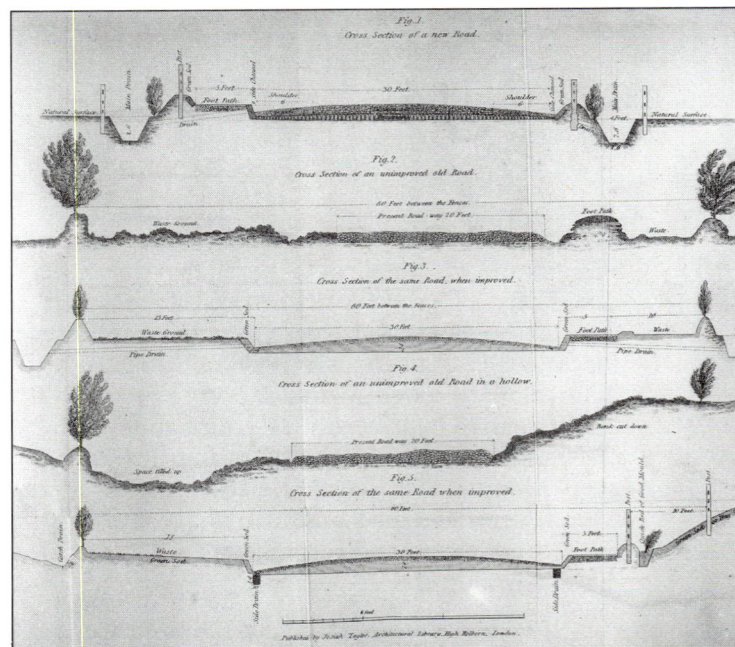

Diagrams used by Telford to illustrate his instructions in *General Rules for Repairing Roads* (see Source A)

Telford gave these instructions to the men in charge of the different sections of the London–Holyhead road. About the same time John Loudon McAdam wrote his instructions for road repairs.

1. Compare the two sets of instructions and list the differences you can find.
2. How would you summarise the differences between a McAdam road and a Telford road?
3. Which would be cheaper to make and keep in good repair?

A1 Telford

Where a road has not a solid and dry foundation, it should be constructed anew. Upon the bottom of it, a pavement should be made 7 inches deep in the middle and 3 inches at the ends. Soft stones will answer. This pavement should be carefully set by hand, with the broadest end of the stones down; the cavities should be filled with stone chips, to make all level and firm, and no stone should be more than 5 inches broad on its face. Over the 18 centre feet of this pavement, 6 inches of stone, or of pebbles of the hardest quality, broken of a size that will in their largest dimensions, pass through a ring of 2½ inches diameter should be laid. The 6 feet of the road, on each side of the 18 centre feet (making in all 30 feet) may be laid with good clean gravel.

General Rules for Repairing Roads, published by order of the Parliamentary Commissioners for the improvement of the mail coach roads from London to Holyhead, new edition, 1827

A2 McAdam

The stone in the road is to be loosed up to the depth of a foot, and broken so as to pass through a screen or harp of an inch in the opening, by which no stone above an inch in any of its dimensions can be admitted.

The road is then to be laid as flat as possible, if it is not hollow in the middle it is sufficient; the less it is rounded the better; water cannot stand upon a level surface.

The broken stone is then to be laid evenly on it, but if half or six inches is laid on first, and exposed a short time to the pressure of carriages, and then a second coat of six inches laid on, it has been found advantageous in consolidating the materials.

A rake of iron with short teeth . . . is to be employed by a *careful* man, in raking the track crossways when the road is first used; this will fill the tracks at once and keep the road level. Tracks will not appear again after the road has settled, the whole mass will become like one solid smooth surfaced stone.

J. McAdam, *Observations on the Highways of the Kingdom*, Parliamentary Papers, 1810–11

McAdam

John Loudon McAdam was also a Scot, but his family were landowners in a small way. He emigrated to America but returned when the American colonies broke with Britain in 1783. He found it hard to find a new career until he started to investigate turnpike trusts and methods of road repair. He later claimed that he had travelled 30,000 miles doing this. It paid off in 1816 when he was made surveyor to the Bristol Turnpike Trust, at the age of sixty. It was the ideal place to put his ideas in to action because the Trust was a large one with 149 miles of road.

McAdam believed that making roads to Telford's high standards was an unnecessary expense. Almost any surface could take a sound highway if the work was carefully supervised. This was good news for turnpike trusts because it meant that their old roads could be improved cheaply. You had workmen lift the old covering, sift out any soft dirt, break up the large stones to less then an inch and relay the road without the expense of going to a quarry for new materials.

Two people were essential to success. One was a supervisor to see that repairs were carried out quickly with the right materials laid in the right way. The other was the stone breaker. A typical sight on one of McAdam's roads was the heaps of broken stones and every now and then a seated worker, often a woman, breaking stones with a hammer.

McAdam believed that most trusts were too small to pay for well-qualified supervisors. He was in favour of making them amalgamate so that a few larger ones would each control many more miles. Trusts were not keen to give up their local powers but many did the next best thing. Several trusts in one district each appointed McAdam or one of his sons so that all their roads were supervised by inspectors trained by the McAdams. The year after his death in 1836, his sons were working for fifty-eight trusts.

Road workers in 1814. Would they be more likely to be working for Telford or McAdam? Why?

A

A1 An advertisement of 1731.

A2 An advertisement of the 1820s for the coach services from the small town of Cheltenham.

Early Coaching Bill.
(Reduced in facsimile from the original, in the possession of John Suffield, Esq.)

BIRMINGHAM STAGE-COACH,

In Two *Days* and a half; begins *May* the 24th, 1731.

SETS out from the *Swan-Inn* in *Birmingham*, every *Monday* at six a Clock in the Morning, through *Warwick*, *Banbury* and *Alesbury*, to the *Red Lion Inn* in *Aldersgate street, London*, every *Wednesday* Morning: And returns from the said *Red Lion Inn* every *Thursday* Morning at five a Clock the same Way to the *Swan-Inn* in *Birmingham* every *Saturday*, at 21 Shillings each Passenger, and 18 Shillings from *Warwick*, who has liberty to carry 14 Pounds in Weight, and all above to pay *One Penny a Pound*.

Perform'd (if God permit)

By Nicholas Rothwell.

The Weekly Waggon sets out every *Tuesday* from the *Nagg's-Head* in Birmingham, to the *Red Lion Inn* aforesaid, every *Saturday*; and returns from the said Inn every *Monday*, to the *Nagg's-Head* in Birmingham every *Thursday*.

Note. By the said Nicholas Rothwell at Warwick, all Persons may be furnished with a By-Coach, Chariot, Chaise, or Hearse, with a Mourning Coach and able Horses, to any Part of Great Britain, at reasonable Rates: And also Saddle Horses to be had.

PLOUGH HOTEL COACH OFFICE, (Cheltenham.)
ROYAL MAILS AND LIGHT & ELEGANT POST COACHES
DAILY TO THE FOLLOWING PLACES.

1. What do these tell you about the a) frequency of services b) the number of places served regularly
2. Use the illustrations to list the changes in the design and haulage of coaches between these years.

B

London–Manchester		London–Edinburgh	
1754	4 days	1750	10 days
1784	2 days		(12 in winter)
1836	29 hours	1836	45½ hours

London–Birmingham	
1731	1 coach per week
1783	30 coaches per week
1829	34 coaches per day

Average no of passengers	
1750	4 inside + 4 outside
1830	4 inside + 11–14 outside

3. Summarise what these tables tell you about the coaching revolution from the 1750s to the 1830s?
4. Average road journey times in the 1950s were calculated at about thirty miles in an hour. By the 1980s sixty miles was common. How do these changes compare with those of the 1750s–1830s?

The mail coach

The most rapid changes in stage-coach services came from the 1780s on. One reason was the example set by the Post Office when it gave way to pressure from Samuel Palmer, a theatre owner in Bath. He worked out a scheme to replace the post-boys with coaches which would carry the mail and a few passengers. Mail would have the priority. There would be an armed guard who was responsible for the mail, not the passengers. If the coach broke-down the guard had to take one of the horses and ride on with the mail. To speed the mail, toll-gate keepers would be bound by law to have the gates open when they heard the guard's horn.

The Post Office did not like the scheme which meant changes in its traditional way of doing things. Then in 1784 the new Prime Minister, William Pitt (twenty-four years old), ordered it to change over and make Palmer head of the mail service – a job he did rather badly. Yet the service lasted as he designed it until trains began to carry the mail. The Post Office never owned the coaches. They were hired from a London coach builder, John Vidler, who supplied the drivers and was responsible for cleaning and servicing the coaches. In 1811 there were 220 regular mail-coach services, twenty-eight of them leaving London daily at eight o'clock sharp in the evening. Passengers were charged about twice the ordinary coach fare and the number of outside passengers was never more than seven.

The stage coach

Mail-coaches were only a small part of the coaching system. By the 1830s London had about 600 services and there were about 3,300 in the country altogether. There were fifty per day between Bristol and Bath. To keep the coaches running, 150,000 horses were needed. Coaches usually changed horses every ten miles or so, and needed five horses for each of these stages. Each day, one was resting while the other four did about one hour's hard work, pulling a coach with up to seventeen passengers and their luggage for about ten miles.

Reaching 10 miles per hour was one of the triumphs of the age. Just as car travel was calculated at 30 mph in the 1940s and 60 mph in the 1980s, so travel times in the 1780s was reckoned at 4–5 mph compared with 9–10 in the 1830s. In both cases, the reasons were partly to do with road improvements and partly in vehicle design. Coaches were made larger but also lighter and lower with less danger of over-turning.

All stage-coach services were connected with inns. Coaching inns had to be large enough to stable many horses and well organised enough to change the teams in no more than five minutes. In the large towns, inn owners were often also coach service operators. The giant of coaching was William Chaplin who owned London's busiest coaching inn, the Swan with Two Necks, and five other London coaching inns. In 1838 he had 2,000 employees, 1,800 horses and 64 coaches.

Coaches and the economy

Canal and coach services developed side by side and each had their place in the industrial revolution. Wherever there was a choice of carrying heavy goods by canal or road, the waterways were always much cheaper so freight on the roads increased very little. Yet roads could compete when it came to light goods. In about 1815 Pickfords started a new service of 'caravans on springs and guarded'. Other carriers also started similar fly-van services which were an ideal way of sending packages and small quantities of goods which were needed quickly.

The coaches assisted trade and industry in many ways. You could send a letter overnight from London to Manchester and it would arrive in time for a reply to be put on the night coach. So legal business, arrangements for lending money and orders for goods were speeded up. Using the stage coaches, salesmen could travel to customers, or engineers go to inspect new buildings or

machinery in a quarter of the time it would have taken by horseback.

Coaches made 'news' possible. Before their day it had often been called 'intelligence' (meaning information). Now it could be really new. Mail-coach guards were given announcements of important events (such as the victory at Waterloo) to call out at each stopping place. London papers, such as *The Times* which started steam-printing in 1807, could be read in other towns. Most people, however, read local papers. These were now able to print information sent by coach about shipping, or the price of raw materials in the great exchanges in the big cities where wool, cotton, and metals were sold.

C

A mail coach schedule for the London to Carlisle run in 1797. By the 1830s the journey would take nearer 45 hours.

The first column shows the contractor, often an inn-keeper, who was responsible for the changes of horse. D meant 'distance' and TA meant 'time available'. The times of arrival are by the local clock unless they are marked TP which was the guard's timepiece which was set to London time.

London to Carlisle

	D.	T.A.		No. 12
			G.P.O. 8	P.M.
Wilson	27	3.35	Redburne 11.35	,,
Goode	8	1. 5	Dunstable 12.40	A.M.
Levi	33	4.40 30	Northampton 5.20 (T.P.), *Breakfast 30 m*	,,
Benton	32	4.20	Leicester 10.10 (T.P.)	,,
Holland	28	3.45 30	Derby 1.55, *Dinner 30 mins*	P.M.
Wallis & Houghton	13	1.45	Ashbourne 4.10 (T.P.)	,,
Hargrave	15	2.10 15	Leek 6.20, *Refreshment 15 m*	,,
Goodwin	13	1.45	Macclesfield 8.20	,,
Pickford	20	2.35	Manchester 10.55 (T.P.)	,,
		4. 5	'To depart precisely at Three o'Clock in the Morning'	A.M.
Paterson	11	1.50	Hulton Lane 4.50	,,
Middlehurst	11	1.40	Chorley 6.30	,,
Cooper	10	1.25 30	Preston 7.55, O.B. 30 mins	,,
,,	22	3.10 10	Lancaster 11.35, O.B. 10 mins (T.P.)	,,
Rigg	11	1.25	Burton 1.10	P.M.
Masterson	11	1.25 40	Kendal 2.35, *Dinner 40 mins*	,,
Gibson	15	2.30	Shap 5.45	,,
Buchanan	11	1.30	Penrith 7.15	,,
Wilson & Fairbairne	18	2.45	P.O. Carlisle 10	,,
	309	50. 0		

5. How much time could passengers spend out of the coach?
6. What is the average time per mile for the journey including stops?
7. At what speed did the coach travel, excluding all possible stops?
8. Is this a journey you would have wanted to make? Explain your answer.

Interpreting pictures

A scene painted outside Nottingham.

1. Approximately when do you think this picture was painted? Give your reasons.
2. What is the building on the left of the road?
3. Which set of passengers would use the road free – why?
   Which might very well resent paying – why?
4. Can you explain why the canal bridge is a) hump-backed; b) has low walls?

Knowledge and understanding

1. From this Part find two sources which illustrate each of these statements. For each source explain why you have chosen it:
   a) heavy goods transport was cheaper by canal than road;
   b) there were important links between the iron industry and canals;
   c) up to the 1750s the main result of turnpiking was to improve goods carriage. After that date, their main importance was in improving passenger travel.

2. How many comparisons can you find between James Brindley and Thomas Telford – in their background, their methods of working and their achievements?

3. Note down five points you would make to support the view that the early industrial revolution could not have taken place without the changes described in this Part.

Before you read Part Four

This Part takes the story up to about 1830, but canals remained an important means of carrying heavy goods throughout the nineteenth century. Turnpike trusts suffered more from the coming of railways because they lost the chance of collecting tolls from stage-coach services. Many fell into debt and the work was often taken over by parishes again. Then in the 1880s and 1890s the new county councils and district councils were made responsible (as they are today) for most roads. In 1900 there were hardly any more roads than there were in the 1830s. Macadamising, as McAdam's technique was called, remained the usual way of making the surface until the motor car when the stones needed to be mixed with tar to stop dust and the roads from breaking up.

4

THE RAILWAY AGE

When public railways began in 1830, there was soon a massive change in the scale of building, speed of travel and amount of freight that could be carried.

A From plateway to public railway – the background to the Liverpool and Manchester Railway
B Engineers and navvies – the men who made the early railways
C A national system – the railway mania and developments in the 1840s
D Living in the early railway age
E Skills section: using longer documents

A bridge of the turnpike era – Ironbridge

Scale

Length of rail in use:

1825	26.75 miles
1830	97.50 miles
1835	335.75 miles
1840	1,497.75 miles
1845	2,441.00 miles
1850	6,084.00 miles

A bridge of the railway era – Newcastle

Speed

Fastest journeys from London, c.1851

City	Time
Bath	2½ hours
Manchester	5 hours
Edinburgh	11½ hours

Background

Pig-iron production

1825	580,000 tons
1830	400,000 tons
1840	1,396,400 tons
1850	2,250,000 tons

Coal output

1830	22.5 million tons
1840	30.0 million tons
1850	49.5 million tons

Steam power in use

1800	20,000 h.p.
1824	100,000 h.p.
1850	500,000 h.p.

Before you read on:

a) Compare the tables on this page with those on page 19 and source B, page 28. How would you summarise the differences?
b) Look back at map E in Unit 3B. What does this suggest about the sort of districts where steam railways were likely to be first used?

Platelayers

Today the person who lays or mends railway track is a 'platelayer'. In the late eighteenth century that was just what he did on the waggonways which linked coalmines and ironworks to the nearest water. The first rails had been wood until, in 1767, the Coalbrookdale ironworks made cast-iron plates which could be laid on top. Iron plates quickly became standard for a good reason: a horse could haul ten tonnes along them compared with only two on a wooden rail.

In the early nineteenth century, the plates gave way to all-iron rails laid on top of wooden or stone sleepers. You could find these tracks called plateways, waggonways or tramways wherever there were heavy goods, but the two biggest networks were in South Wales (see map E, Unit 3B) and the pits of north-east England.

A

Map of tramways in north-east England.

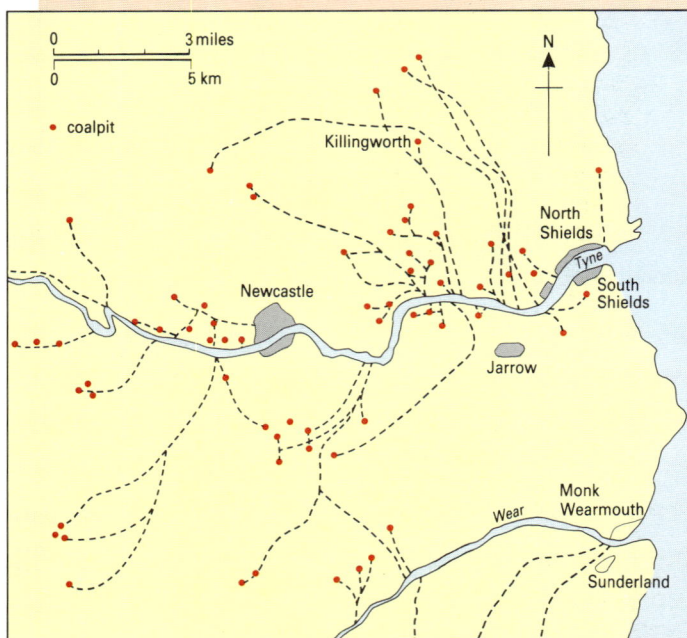

1. What does this suggest about the importance of the iron industry to transport by the early 1800s?

Steampower

Thomas Newcomen made his first steam 'atmospheric' engine in 1712 and many coalmines used them for pumping out water. In 1775 the first Boulton and Watt engines appeared. They were much more efficient and could soon drive wheels and machinery. Collieries installed them to haul men and coal from the bottom of pit-shafts and then to haul waggons up the slope or inclines on their waggonways.

With steam engines came new jobs. George Stephenson was the son of a Tyneside pitworker. He first worked as a fireman, stoking boilers before he was promoted to brakeman in charge of a steam engine. In 1812 he became engineer to a group of mines around Killingworth in charge of all their engines and their waggonways.

Putting steam on wheels

Boulton and Watt patented their engine which meant it could not be legally copied until 1800 when many inventors were ready with ideas to improve it. Richard Trevithick, a Cornish mines engineer, believed that Watt was too cautious when he made engines with pressure of no more than five pounds to the square inch. Trevithick showed that ten times as much pressure was safe. The result was a lighter and much smaller engine. From here it was only a small step to put one on wheels.

In 1804 the owner of the Penydarren ironworks at Merthyr Tydfil bet £500 that Trevithick's engine could haul ten tons of iron on the 9¾ miles of tramway to the Glamorgan canal (see Map E Unit 3B). Trevithick won him his bet, although his engine did a lot of damage to the track. The few passengers who travelled with the iron had made the first locomotive journey in history.

After that the locomotive moved north. In 1805 the Wylam colliery on Tyneside had a copy of Trevithick's engine. There was still the problem of damage to the track. A Leeds man, John Blenkinsop, found one answer in 1812 with an engine which had a central cogged wheel to pull it along a cogged rail. For several years these engines pulled up to thirty waggons of coal along the 3½ miles from Middleton Colliery into Leeds.

B

A painting of the Leeds Colliery which appeared in a book published in 1814 called *Costumes of Yorkshire*.

2. How is the engine recognisable as Blenkinsop's?
3. What other use of steam power can be seen?

The cogged rails and wheels were too expensive for the longer waggonways on Tyneside. The Wylam colliery tried again in 1813 with William Hedley's *Wylam Dilly*. George Stephenson followed in 1814 with *Blucher* – named after the Prussian general who was playing a leading part in bringing Napoleon to his heels. From this time, Stephenson's main interest was in railways. In 1815 he built another locomotive and invented a new way of joining iron rails. Between 1819 and 1822 he built a complete new waggonway which had stationary engines winding trucks up the inclines and five locomotives. In the next year with the help of Edward Pease, a businessman from Darlington, he and his son, Robert, opened a works to make locomotives in Newcastle.

The Stockton & Darlington

Edward Pease was one of a group of businessmen from Stockton and Darlington who met in 1810 to discuss a way of bringing coals from the mines, which were twenty miles inland, to their towns. They had several surveys made to decide whether it should be canal or rail. By 1821 they had agreed on rail and it was natural that they should choose George Stephenson to build it.

The single 25½ mile track was made of 5½ metres-long wrought-iron rails. They came from a rolling mill of the sort invented by Henry Cort, and were far tougher than the short cast-iron lengths used earlier. At the western end there were two steep inclines with stationary engines to haul waggons up. Between them, waggons were hauled by horses. For the rest of the journey the track would take waggons drawn by either horse or locomotive. The stationary engines and the locomotives were built by Robert Stephenson & Co.

The line opened on 27th September with George Stephenson at the wheel of *Locomotion* pulling twenty-one coal waggons, fitted with benches for the day. Nearly 600 people struggled on board. With a few stops for repairs, it arrived in Stockton at an average speed of about 6 mph. Behind came twenty-four waggons each pulled by a horse. After that the Stockton and Darlington settled down to be a railway mostly for coal. Some was carried in waggons hauled by the company's locomotives but more was in horse-drawn waggons whose owners paid a toll to use the track. It was the first public railway but it was only a short step on from a private waggonway.

The Liverpool & Manchester

C

Prospectus of the Liverpool & Manchester Railroad Company, 1824.

> The total quantity of merchandise passing between Liverpool and Manchester is estimated by the lowest computation at one thousand tons per day. The bulk of this merchandise is transported either by the Duke of Bridgewater's canal or the 'Mersey and Irwell Navigation'... The average length of passage... may be taken at 36 hours...
>
> By the projected railroad, the transit of merchandise between Liverpool and Manchester will be effected in four or five hours, and the charge to the merchant will be reduced at least one third... for travellers the railway holds out the prospect... the magnitude and importance of which cannot be immediately ascertained.

4. Describe the two main gains that the promoters expected. What were they less certain about?

In 1827 George Stephenson was made engineer of the new railway. His first challenge was the swamp known as Chat Moss which other engineers said would never take the weight. He instructed the men to ram in brushwood and heather and to lay open tarred barrels to form a drain. Then they dumped dried moss week after week until a firm embankment appeared.

By 1829 the line was nearly complete but the directors were still debating the way it should be used. One seriously suggested having stationary engines every mile or so to wind the waggons along. Stephenson persuaded them to hold trials and offer £500 to the engine which performed best over a level 1¾ miles. There were four entries and the trials at Rainhill took seven days. The winner was the *Rocket*, made by Robert Stephenson & Co, which managed speeds up to 29 mph. The Rainhill trials made three things certain. First, the Company would use locomotives. Second, toll-paying users could not be allowed on tracks which had engines running at 29 mph. When the railway opened in 1830 the company itself managed all the trains. Third, with such speeds, the railway had a very good chance of putting stage coaches out of business.

D

The Liverpool & Manchester in 1831.

5. In which different workshops would the carriages have been made?

A

The Liverpool & Manchester after 1½ years.

Before the establishment of the Liverpool and Manchester railway, there were twenty-two regular and about seven occasional extra coaches between these places which, in full, could only carry per day 688 persons. The railway, from its commencement, carried 700,000 persons in eighteen months being an average of 1070 a day. It has not been stopped for a single day. The fare by coach was 10s inside and 5s outside – by railway it is 5s inside and 3s 6d outside. The time occupied in making the journey by coach was four hours – by railway it is one hour and three quarters. All the coaches but one have ceased running. . . Goods delivered in Manchester the same day they are received in Liverpool. By canal they were never delivered before the third day. . . The savings to manufacturers in the neighbourhood of Manchester, in the carriage of cotton alone, has been £20,000 per annum.

Annual Register, 1832

1. Compare this extract with the Company's prospectus in 3A. Would they have changed their views about the railway's value?

The Liverpool & Manchester railway turned out quite differently from the Stockton & Darlington. Instead of a public waggonway for goods moving at 5 or 6 mph it was mainly a passenger service carrying people at up to 30 mph. Profits began to come in even before the company had built branch lines and sidings to cope with heavy freight. The chance of profit meant that it was easy to issue shares to start new railway companies. By the end of the 1830s Parliament had passed Acts for nearly 2,000 miles of railway.

Many leading road and bridge engineers hoped to be given the chance to build the new railways, but most companies turned to the men behind the success of the Liverpool & Manchester. For nearly every company, the engineer was either George or Robert Stephenson, or someone who had worked with them such as John Locke, an assistant engineer on the Liverpool & Manchester.

Robert Stephenson: the London & Birmingham

Robert Stephenson had the most important post, as engineer to the London & Birmingham Railway. In 1831–2 he made a survey, looking for the route which had the gentlest gradients. The rest of 1832, and half of 1833, was taken up with the struggle to get MPs to pass an Act against the opposition of canal and stage-coach companies, and against landowners along the way. Many of the landowners were encouraged to agree by being paid three times that which the Company had budgeted.

Once the Act was passed in 1833, Robert Stephenson divided the 112 miles into twenty-nine sections. Some were lengths of track of about six miles and the rest were special works such as bridges and tunnels. The work on each one was given to a contractor. The sections were all to be built at the same time and for four years there were between 12,000 and 20,000 men at work. Some contractors sub-divided their sections among sub-contractors. They provided the wheelbarrows, picks and shovels and horses, and hired gangs of navvies to do the hard work.

'Navvy' came from 'navigator', the name first given to a labourer who dug canals. He was a different type of person from the general farm labourer or the casual town worker. He had to be able to keep up with the rest of his gang which was usually on piece work. One contractor's timekeeper described them:

I think as fine a spectacle as any man could witness. . .is to see a cutting in full operation, with about twenty waggons being filled, every man at his post, and every man with his shirt open, working in the heat of the day, the gangers looking about and everything going like clockwork.

It needed strength to keep this rhythm going. The standard for a shovelman was to load fourteen tonnes of earth or rock a day. If it was needed for an embankment it would go into waggons and be taken away. If not, it went into a runner's wheelbarrow. Up the sides of the cuttings were wooden plankways with a pulley at the top. A rope was tied to the barrow and to a horse on the other side of the pulley. The runner gave a signal and the horse pulled, drawing the barrow up the muddy plank with the runner stopping it slipping off sideways or sliding back if the horse slowed down.

After a day's work the navvy went back with the gang to the camp of tents or rough wooden huts that was home for a year or more until the gang moved to a new job. He was not accepted as a true navvy unless he could manage to eat like one: 0.8 kg of beef and 3½ litres of beer were common quantities. Once a month the ganger was paid and he shared out the earnings which were often not all in cash. There were laws against paying 'truck' in factories, but not on the railways. 'Truck' meant paying in goods or tokens. Many sub-contractors gave tickets which could only be used in their tommy-shops in exchange for food, which was often bad, and drink, which was often watered.

A camp of hundreds of navvies was a terrifying experience for peaceful villages along the route. The terror started with the strange accents of the navvies who were often from Ireland, Scotland or the Yorkshire

The dangers of navvy work were illustrated in a report on safety published in 1840.

2. Navvies were killed so often that at first no inquests were held on their deaths. What dangers was the illustrator trying to show at points A to G?

3. How would an illustration of a motorway works show different methods of work, and different dangers?

dales. Hardly any had families with them, which meant anxious times for the parents of village girls. Paydays were often followed by a bout of drunkenness which could go on for several days.

The largest and longest navvy camp on the London & Birmingham was at Kilsby where Robert Stephenson planned a tunnel 2,195 metres long. The contractor dug sixteen shafts so that navvies could mine each way from the bottom of each one. But the shafts ended in waterlogged quicksand, and flooded. The contractor gave up and Robert Stephenson moved in himself with 1,200 men. They built a railway to shift equipment and made thirteen narrow shafts each with a huge pumping engine at the top. The pumps worked for nineteen months, pumping 6,800 litres-a-minute before the quicksand was drained and tunnelling could begin.

I.K. Brunel: the Great Western Railway

On 5 December 1831, a traveller on the Liverpool & Manchester let his pencil make squiggles and wavy lines on a piece of paper as the train rattled along. He put the paper in his diary and added a note:

> I record this specimen of the shaking on the Manchester railway. The time is not far off when we shall be able to take our coffee and write while going noiselessly and smoothly at 45 miles per hour – let me try.

The man was Isambard Kingdom Brunel. He was an engineer already known for his flair in coming up with new ideas. In the early 1830s he was working in Bristol on designs for a suspension bridge and on new docks. They were to be part of Bristol's efforts to win back some of the trade lost to Liverpool. In 1833 four Bristol business-men formed the 'Great Western Railway Company' to link their town with London, and made Brunel their engineer.

He was the first railway builder who had never worked on any scheme with the Stephensons and he set out to surpass their efforts. When the line was finished in 1841 it was a magnificent affair with bridges and stations all designed by Brunel himself. Where the Box Tunnel left Bath, he built a classical archway to match the town's architecture.

Brunel wanted faster and more powerful engines, and smoother-running carriages than any built so far. He persuaded the Company to ignore the 'coal-waggon' gauge of 4 feet 8½ inches (1.42 m) used everywhere else and lay tracks 7 feet-wide to carry the new engines.

When the London–Bristol line was finished the GWR began to build branch lines northwards. In 1844 one reached Gloucester. From the other direction passengers and freight from the whole of the north and midlands reached the town by the narrow-gauge Birmingham & Gloucester line. There was daily chaos at the station – and the 'battle of the gauges' was on. Was Bristol and the whole of the south and south-west to be cut off from the railways of the rest of the country?

Railways and their passengers

A

Second class, Eastern Counties Railway, 1847.

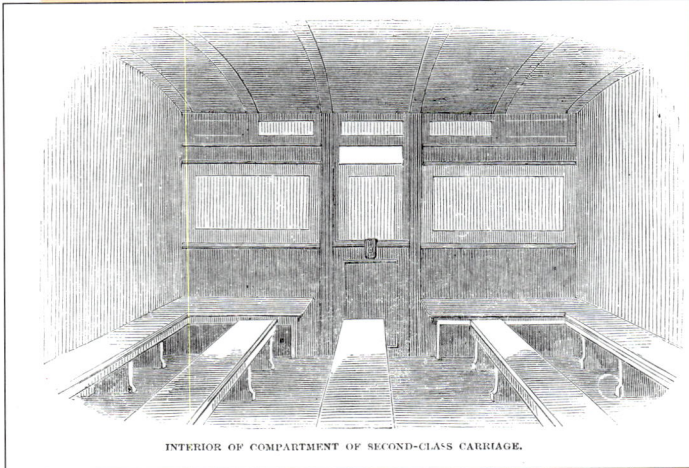

INTERIOR OF COMPARTMENT OF SECOND-CLASS CARRIAGE.

1. What would a person who used to travel outside a coach be likely to think of his accommodation in 1847?
2. Look back to Source D in Unit 4A. How does this compartment compare with the second class accommodation?

First-class travellers were the old inside-coach passengers. They got curtained windows and padded seats, four to a compartment with sometimes a two seater at the front. Their luggage went on top and the guard sat where he had done on a stage coach. The outside-coach passenger travelled second class. It was not luxurious but, at half the cost and twice the speed of the coach, it was a good bargain.

Third-class passengers were people who would never have travelled by coach and the early railways were barely interested in them. They provided open waggons without seats, springs or buffers. Most were connected to goods trains and often only ran at night.

Train journeys could be dangerous. Signalling was primitive. On the Liverpool & Manchester it was done by men with hand lamps and flags. In 1834 they moved to boards which swung over the track to order a train to stop. In 1841 the Great Western jumped ahead with tall posts with a disc for 'go' and a bar for 'stop'. These simple methods did not always stop train accidents, when third-class passengers came off worst.

The government and the railways

The government set its face against copying the French and Belgians who built state railway lines over the important routes. But it stepped in over safety and the treatment of third-class passengers. The 1840 Railways Regulation Act set up inspectors to check new lines and to keep records of accidents. This was followed in 1844 by the Railway Act.

B

B1

Railway Companies...shall by means of one train at the least to travel along their railway from one end to the other of each trunk, branch or junction line...once at the least on every week day... provide for the conveyance of Third Class passengers...The carriages in which passengers shall be conveyed by such train shall be provided with seats and shall be protected from the weather. The fare or charge shall not exceed one penny for each mile travelled.

Railway Act, 1884

B2 Inside a parliamentary train.

3. What does this picture tell you about the social effects of the 1844 Act?

The Railway Mania

By 1844 there were 2,044 miles in service and another 1,000 being built. Some thought that was enough and attacked the greed of the people who joined in the 'mania' which swept the country between 1845 and 1847. In three years, MPs passed 330 Railway Acts and turned down 600 which were mostly pipe-dreams or dishonest attempts to get investors to part with money.

In just a few years the railway mania led to the greatest change ever made to the English landscape. At its peak, 250,000 people were at work on embankments, cuttings, viaducts and stations. Over a quarter of all the pig-iron produced was made into railway line. When most of the lines were laid by 1851, there were 6,800 miles in service. London was linked to Wales, Ireland (via Holyhead) and to Scotland (with two lines).

The mania forced the government to step into the battle of the gauges. When it realised broad tracks might reach as far north as Wolverhampton, three Commissioners were ordered to make an enquiry. They ran trials which showed that the best speed of a narrow-gauge train pulling fifty tons was 53¾ mph while a broad-gauge locomotive hauled eighty tons at 60 mph. The Commission wrote that 'the public are mainly indebted for the present rate of speed and the increased accommodation of the railway carriages to the genius of Mr. Brunel'. But they decided that times and costs would suffer if there were more meetings between the two systems. In 1846 the Gauge Act said that all railways except for the Great Western and lines to its south should be 4 feet 8½ inches (or 5 feet 3 inches in Ireland). The Great Western kept to the broad gauge until 1892, but their branch lines had an inside rail for narrow-gauge trains.

As traffic increased it was clear that there were other obstacles to a smooth running network. Passengers and freight often travelled over several railways all charging different prices. Some of the leading companies came together in a 'clearing house' which began to arrange through-rates and fares from 1842. Another solution was to amalgamate. In 1846–7 around fifty companies formed themselves into just nine. One of the most important amalgamations came in 1846 when the three pioneering lines built by the Stephensons joined to form the London & North Western Railway.

'King' Hudson

On the other side of the country amalgamations made a short-lived fortune for a York draper. George Hudson had no technical knowledge of railways but used a legacy to buy shares and become Chairman of the North Midland Railway. It carried people and goods from the iron and textile towns of Yorkshire as far as Derby. Here its trains ended up in the same station as the lines of the Midland Counties and the Birmingham to Derby railways. Each wanted the trade from Derby to London via Rugby. A price war followed in which both companies nearly ruined themselves. In 1844, George Hudson bought them both and joined them with the North Midland to make a single Midland Railway.

By 1849 Hudson had bought up or amalgamated so many companies that he was spoken of as 'the railway king'. He was also an MP and living in great luxury. Then suspicious shareholders had his books investigated. They showed that money had gone into his own pocket and that he had paid high dividends to shareholders with the cash that others had paid for shares in different Hudson companies. He was bankrupt after repaying some of the money and would have gone to a debtors' prison but for the fact that he was an MP.

C

A map showing the extent of railways by 1851.

6. Explain how George Hudson's railways and the London & North Western were each well placed to carry goods from the leading centres of industry.

7. Find four towns on the map which were not centres of industry but became important as railway junctions.

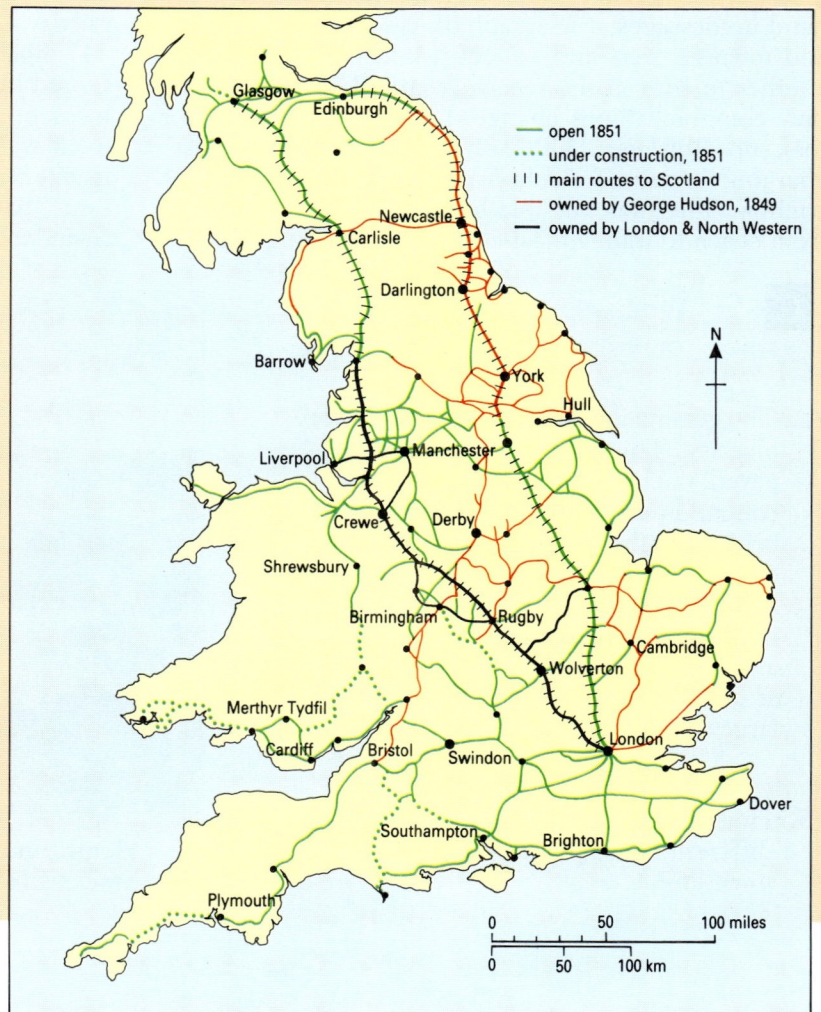

D LIVING IN THE EARLY RAILWAY AGE

A change of pace

A

People who breakfast in York and dine in London – who may be summoned from Liverpool to the Metropolis in three or four minutes by the electric telegraph and answer the summons in person within six or seven hours by the express train – acquire a habit of pressure and velocity in all they do.

William Johnston, *Britain as It Is*, 1851

1. Explain how William Johnston believes that some peoples' lives are changed by railways.

In the 1850s the average journey time (including stops) for an ordinary train was 20 mph. The 1844 Act forced companies to see the value of third-class passengers and almost all trains had coaches for them. Express trains, for first and second class only, travelled at an average of about 40 mph – four times the speed of stage coaches. Safety at such speeds was helped by the electric telegraph, invented by Cooke and Wheatstone in 1835. Brunel laid it along the GWR in 1838 and other railways followed. By the 1850s, signalmen could use it to send all-clear messages for each block of line.

The telegraph also became a public service. You could hand in messages at telegraph offices in railway stations and town centres, and a clerk would tap them out for another to copy at the receiving end. This was not the only communications change. In 1841 the Post Office took up Rowland Hill's scheme for a 'penny post', charging the same for delivering letters to any part of the country. That was possible because they changed over from coach to train almost as soon as each line opened.

Standardising time

B

London time is about four minutes earlier than Reading time, seven and a half minutes before Cirencester and 14 minutes before Bridgewater.

GWR Timetable, July 1841

2. Why was London time different from some other towns'?

The first railway to use London time throughout was the LNWR. Soon all station clocks showed London or 'railway time' and so did telegraph and post offices. In 1880 it became Greenwich Mean Time by law.

Railways and towns

Railways made living conditions much worse in many industrial towns. The companies bought up houses to make room for their stations, sidings and viaducts. Landlords made handsome profits but no-one built replacement homes for the tenants. Overcrowding in houses without water and w.c.s became worse.

The other side of the picture was the new towns built by railway companies. In 1841 Crewe was a village with 247 inhabitants but four railway lines met there and the Grand Junction decided that it was an ideal place for its locomotive and carriage works. The result was a model town with well laid-out streets, churches and schools, teachers and doctors. The LNWR built another on the same pattern at Wolverton. The GWR built 'New Swindon' alongside the old town of Old Swindon.

C

C1

The general appearance of Crewe is very pleasing. The streets are wide and well-paved; the houses are very neat and commodious, usually of two stories, built of bricks, but the bricks concealed by rough-cast plaster, with porches, lattice windows and a little piece of garden-ground before the door . . . The accommodation is good, and it would be difficult to find such houses at such low rents even in the suburbs of a large town.

Chambers Journal, 1850

3. How do these two sources illustrate two different consequences of railways for town life?

C2 Homes and factories near the railway viaduct in Stockport in the 1850s.

The railways created some new industrial towns. When the Furness railway reached the village of Barrow in 1847 it had forty-seven inhabitants. The trains brought in coal to smelt the local iron ore and Barrow-in-Furness became one of the great iron towns of the nineteenth century. Middlesborough had 151 inhabitants in 1831. The railway started its growth into a sprawling iron and chemical town. Cardiff was already a small port for coastal ships. When the Taff Valley Railway opened it built new docks to handle steam coal which was exported all over the world.

The Excursion

THE WONDER OF 1851!
FROM YORK
TO LONDON AND BACK FOR A CROWN.

THE MIDLAND RAILWAY COMPANY
Will continue to run

TWO TRAINS DAILY
(Excepted Sunday, when only one Train is available)

FOR THE GREAT EXHIBITION,
UNTIL SATURDAY, OCTOBER 11.

Without any Advance of Payment

RETURN SPECIAL TRAINS leave the Euston Station on MONDAYS, TUESDAYS, THURSDAYS, & SATURDAYS at 11 a.m., on WEDNESDAYS and FRIDAYS at 1 p.m., and EVERY NIGHT (Sundays excepted) at 9 p.m.
First and Second Class Tickets are available for returning any day (except Sunday) up to and including Monday, Oct. 20. Third Class Tickets issued before the 6th instant are available for 14 days, and all issued after the 6th are returnable any day up to Monday the 20th.
The Trains leave York at 9-40 a.m. every day except Sunday, and also every day, including Sunday, at 7-20 p.m.

Fares to London and Back :—
1st Class 15s. 2nd, 10s, 3rd, 5s.
The Midland is the only Company that runs Trains Daily at these Fares.
Ask for Midland Tickets!

Children above 3 and under 12 years of age, Half-price. Luggage allowed—112 lbs. to First Class, 100 lbs. to Second, and 56 lbs. to Third Class Passengers.

APPROVED LODGINGS, of all classes, are provided in London for Passengers by Midland Trains. The Agents will give Tickets of reference on application, without charge, and an Office is opened in London, at DONALD's WATERLOO DINING ROOMS, 14, Seymour-street, near Euston Station, where an agent is in regular attendance to conduct parties who go up unprepared with Lodgings.
The Managers have much pleasure in stating that the immense numbers who have travelled under their arrangements have been conducted in perfect safety—indeed in the history of the Midland Lines, no accident, attended with personal injury, has ever happened to an Excursion Train. In conducting the extraordinary traffic of this Great Occasion the first object is to ensure safety, and that object has hitherto been most happily achieved.
With the fullest confidence, inspired by past success, the Conductors have pleasure in urging those who have not yet visited the Exhibition, to avail themselves of the present facilities, and to improve the opportunity which will close on the 11th of October.
All communications respecting the Trains to be addressed to the Managers, for the Company.

John Cuttle & John Calverley, Wakefield;
Thomas Cook, Leicester.

October 2nd, 1851.

T. COOK, PRINTER, 28, GRANBY-STREET, LEICESTER.

4. What does this poster tell you about changes in railway companies' attitudes to poorer passengers?

The first railway excursion was organised in 1831 when 220 Manchester Sunday School teachers had a day out in Liverpool for 3s 4d return, just under half the cost of a single second-class ticket. Other companies soon realised the profits that could be made from excursions. One of the great examples was Brighton: in 1835, coaches took 117,000 passengers from London. The single journey took six hours and cost 21s inside and 12s outside. In the second half of 1846 the railways carried 360,000 passengers on a 2½ hour journey. The second-class fare was 9s 6d and the third-class 5s but the return excursion was 8s.

Many lodging house keepers, theatre managers and so on believed they would do better by sticking to wealthier customers who stayed longer. In the small northern resorts such as Blackpool and Scarborough there were many who felt the same. But in the 1850s day trips helped them change their mind. Later, they began to cater for families who came for the whole holiday or 'wakes' week from the industrial towns.

The Great Exhibition in 1851 was a great triumph for the railway. Altogether 5 million people came to London by train and the LNWR alone carried 750,000. Most made the round trip in one day; from Manchester and Leeds paying 5s (roughly a day's wages for a skilled craftsman).

In 1841 Thomas Cook was a thirty-three-year-old owner of a small business in Loughborough and a keen supporter of the temperance campaign. In 1841 he organised the first package excursion. A thousand temperance supporters paid a shilling for the eleven-mile return journey from Leicester with ham sandwiches, tea, dancing and cricket thrown in. He soon expanded with package trips to Scotland in 1846 and to the Great Exhibition in 1851. After that he began to make deals with European railways and Cook's tours became a common form of middle-class holiday.

Railways and other transporters

Rates per ton, Birmingham to London

Articles	Rates by canal collected and delivered		Rates by railway collected and delivered
	1836	1842	1842
Hardware	60s. 0d	35s. 0d	40s. 0d
Nails	40 . 0	32 . 6	32 . 6
Raw sugar	40 . 0	37 . 6	37 . 6
Tallow	35 . 0	35 . 0	30 . 0
Tea	50 . 0	37 . 6	40 . 0

Report of the Select Committee on Railway Rates and Fares, 1881

5. What was the canal companies' response to the coming of railways?
6. In which ways does this supply evidence about the benefits of railways to the economy as a whole?

Stage coaches were the first to suffer from competition with rail. The last left London in 1846 and Manchester in 1848. The mail-coach office closed in 1854. Canals were slower to lose their trade for two reasons. In the first place, railways could not cope with much freight until they built goods-stations and warehouses. Secondly the canals opened a price-cutting war. It was only in the 1850s that railways under-cut canal prices for all goods, and even then companies with canal-side warehouses often used waterways for another twenty or thirty years.

c) was the main connection between the three tables on this page?
d) Was the main use of steam ships up to 1850?

A SHIPPING BEFORE THE AGE OF STEAM

Eighteenth-century Britain had several hundred ports for sea-going ships. Only a few were prosperous. All round the coast there were ports which were no more than a sheltered cove with a sloping beach. The map on page 41 shows that the best place for a sea-port was a few miles up river. Here there would be wharves or quays for ships to tie up and warehouses to hold imports and exports.

The busiest ports had a 'legal quay'. These stretches of wharf were the only places for loading and unloading goods which were charged import and export duties. Such ports always had a customs house. The largest ports of all usually faced a part of the world which supplied imports to Britain. Hull was the great port of entry for goods from the Baltic such as timber from Norway, iron ore from Sweden and flax from the Baltic coast. Bristol and Glasgow were the main importers of West Indian sugar and tobacco. London had a share in all trades but was also the leading port for tea, spices, raw silk and cotton from the east Indies.

A

The port of Ipswich in 1753. The customs house is behind the second ship from the left.

1. What problems would there be here in a busy sailing season?
2. Like most eighteenth-century ports, the streets are at right-angles to the waterfront? Why?

Overseas shipping

Most goods for overseas were moved in ships of about 200 tonnes with a crew made up of master, his mate, a boatswain (or bo'sun), who was a kind of foreman in charge of rigging, sails and stores, as well as a carpenter and a cook. After them came able-bodied seamen, who spent their lives at sea and were 'able to hand, reef and steer', followed by ordinary seamen who were less skilled and might be casual labour taken on for a voyage. Sailing was better paid than other manual jobs but many seamen were laid up in the winter. Handling sailing ships in bad weather was dangerous work. One piece of evidence for this is that many seamen's hospitals were opened as charities in the eighteenth century. A great problem for merchant seamen was being 'pressed' or 'impressed' into the fighting navy in times of war.

Most crews spent year after year making the same runs. An Atlantic run might be one, or at the most two, crossings each way a year, while a ship could make three or four to Portugal, five to the Baltic and so on. Imports and exports from the same parts of the world were never in balance. Ships often travelled out light or they had to make up a triangular voyage. Boats sailing to bring sugar from the West Indies would stop in Ireland to take on salted beef, pork, butter or cheese or they might go to Germany to pick up wooden staves for making into barrels on the West Indian plantations. There were three or four sided voyages. One went to Newfoundland to pick up dried fish caught by Canadian fishermen, which was taken straight to Spain or Portugal where the ships were loaded with wines to bring back to Britain. The most infamous triangular trade was carrying goods to west Africa, exchanging them for slaves, taking them across the Atlantic and bringing back tobacco or sugar.

Many ships and crews worked in the re-export trade. The Navigation Laws said that products from British colonies had to be brought first to Britain in British ships with mostly British crews. So legal quays were often piled with sugar, tobacco and tea which were then re-exported to European countries after the customs officers had collected duties.

Docks

Exports grew as deeper coal-mines were sunk, and more iron bars, cotton cloth and other manufactured goods were made, while, at the same time, the population rose. The new industries and the extra people created a demand for more imports of raw materials and food. The extra trade meant that many more ships were built but there were also improvements in design. In the early eighteenth century, a ship's tonnage (measured by the weight of material used to make it) was always about a third greater than the tonne's burden it could carry. By the end of the century they could carry their own weight or more.

More trade also meant that merchants built up more regular trading links with their agents overseas. They opened combined offices and warehouses in the larger ports and did less business in the smaller ones. This led to overcrowding at the quayside. Worst affected of all

42

was London. In 1791, 10,112 coasters and 3,463 foreign-going ships used the port – twice as many as forty years before. Few of them could actually tie up at a berth. They had to be unloaded into some of the 3,400 barges or 'lighters' which worked on the river. The lighters had to land many of the goods on the 'legal quay' which was only 395 metres long. The only people who gained from the chaos were the pilferers. A London magistrate explained some of their activities:

In 1802 work started on two docks for the West India trade, one for imports and one for exports. Each could take well over a mile of shipping. Each was surrounded by warehouses and around the whole area there was a wall and a ditch to keep out thieves. In the next twenty-five years many more London docks were built.

Liverpool's story as a port began with Irish meat and cattle. By the early eighteenth century it was importing salt from across the Atlantic and building a share in the slave and sugar trade. But ships had to be unloaded as they lay aground on the sloping shores of the Mersey. In 1715 part of the 'pool', where the Mersey ran inland, was closed in to make the 'Old Dock'. In 1753 Salt-house Dock was added for the salt trade. Then a series of docks were cut into the banks of the Mersey between the high- and low-water lines. By the 1830s the new shore line with its docks stretched for eight kilometres.

Hull, Glasgow and Newcastle also built docks. So did Bristol although she had difficulties in making them wide and deep enough for the larger ships of the early nineteenth century. By then it was becoming vital for a port to have docks which could handle a wide variety of goods. Smaller ports without docks and dealing in only one or two goods were losing trade.

C

The first docks in Liverpool (left) and London.

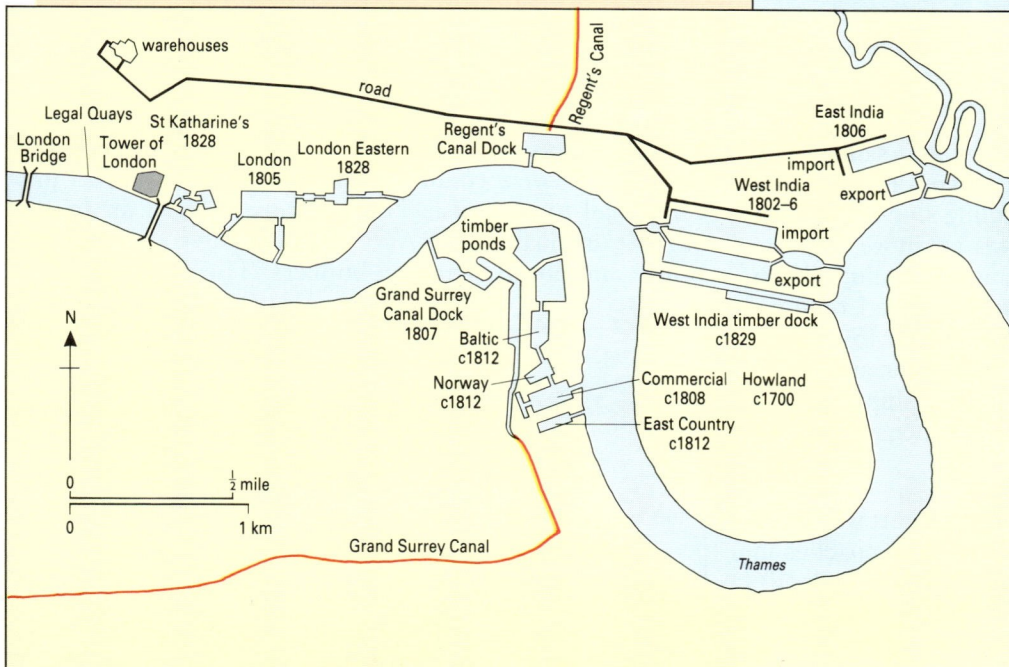

3. Suggest why so many London docks specialised in one part of the world?
4. What does the position of the legal quays tell you about port conditions before the docks were built?
5. What does the high-water line tell you about the problems in building Liverpool's docks?

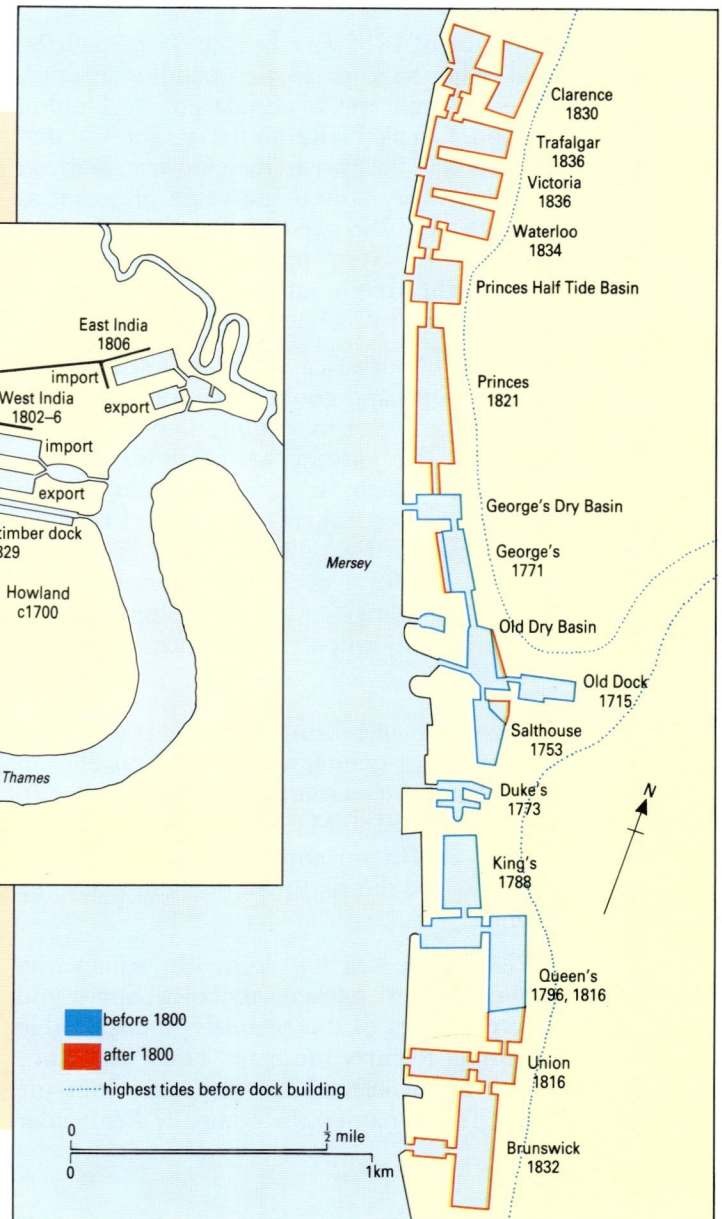

B PADDLES AND SCREWS

The first river services

In the 1790s many people made their way to work in Glasgow by fly-boat (see Unit 3C). By then an American and Frenchman had experimented with steam-driven boats, but the important developments were to come on the Clyde. In 1802 William Symington used a Boulton and Watt engine to turn a wheel at the stern of a boat, the *Charlotte Dundas*. It worked, but the wheel created a great wash and the engine took up most of the room. In 1812 Henry Bell made the *Comet* which had paddles at each side and room for passengers. It was the first successful passenger steamer and the new method of travel became popular almost overnight. Two years later, nine steamboats were running daily services on the Clyde and in the next year the first steam passenger boat was launched on the Thames. In 1842, well over a million passengers made the London–Gravesend journey.

The Packet

The great adventure of 1815 was the round trip made by George Dodd who took a 75-ton paddle steamer, *Thames*, on the 758 mile trip from Glasgow to Dublin, and on to London. Just as the Rainhill trials showed that steam locomotion was the way to develop transport on land, so Dodd's voyage showed the value of steam at sea. By 1821 there were 188 paddle steamers in the seas around Britain. Most were packet steamers which carried parcels, light freight and passengers. Heavy freight was still carried by sailing boat until the 1860s.

A steam packet was about twice as fast as a sailing ship with a favourable wind, and could make a journey in a day which would take a week in a sailing ship if the wind was not favourable. The journey was far more comfortable than by stage coach. Passengers could stretch their legs and need not rush their meals. The London–Edinburgh coach cost £3.10s outside and £6.15s inside, compared with £2.10s for a deck passenger and £4.4s for a cabin, both including food. Packet ship journeys lost their popularity only when railways began to compete in the 1840s.

The seal of approval to new forms of transport was often given by the Post Office (which went over to coaches in 1784, and railways almost as soon as they were opened). In 1821 they began Royal Mail packet services with steam ships between Britain and Ireland. They ran to regular times and were the first mail boats to make the crossing in winter.

In 1835 the Post Office was approached by a man who had just started a steam packet service to Spain and Portugal –· the countries of the Spanish peninsula. He was after a contract to carry the mail. The Post Office gave it to him. Three years later they gave him the service to India. He re-named the company Peninsular and Orient, or P & O, and started to run regular services to Alexandria in Egypt. From Alexandria, passengers and mail went by a combination of Nile boat and horse or carriage across to the Red Sea where they took one of the P & O's boats which took them round India to Calcutta.

The P & O packet boats stopped for coal at British-owned ports such as Gibraltar and Malta. There were no stopping places in the Atlantic and many shipping experts said it was impossible for one ship to carry all the coal its engines would need. There was no proof either way. The only steam power used in the Atlantic had been on ships such as the *Savannah* which crossed in 1819 using her engines for just 3½ days and sails for the other 23.

Brunel's three ships

Isambard Kingdom Brunel said the experts were wrong because every foot you added to ship's length meant an extra *cubic* foot on what it could carry. You just had to build ships larger, and you would find the size which could carry the coal needed. That was the science behind his idea. The commercial idea was more romantic. He was building the Great Western Railway and got the Company to agree that the line need not stop at Bristol. Passengers could go on to America on the new steam ship the *Great Western* that Brunel would build.

He finished it in 1838. It was seventy metres long – compared with the forty-five metres of Nelson's *Victory* – and had two engines driving enormous paddles. As soon as it was built, London shipowners realised that the *Great Western* could win the Post Office contract to carry mail to America. The Londoners hired an Irish sea packet-boat, the *Sirius*, stripped out some of her cabins and put in extra fuel bunkers. The *Sirius* started

The launch of the *Great Britain* at Bristol on 19 July 1843. A lithograph by J Walter.

her crossing from Cork in southern Ireland on 4th April 1838. Four days later the *Great Western* left Bristol. The *Sirius* docked at New York after nineteen days, the first ship to cross by steam only. She had just fifteen tonnes of coal left. A few hours later the *Great Western* steamed in. She had crossed from Bristol in fifteen days, five hours, and had 200 tonnes of coal on board. Brunel had proved his point.

The *Great Western* opened the way to Atlantic steam crossings, although not everything went her owners' way. The Post Office did not give them the mail contract. They had only one ship and it was at the end of the wide-gauge railway. Liverpool was a busier port linked with much more of the country. The contract went to the Canadian, Samuel Cunard, who agreed to build four ships to run a regular service taking eleven to thirteen days. The Cunard line went on to run the world's busiest and smartest liner service but in the 1840s its ships could only carry a few passengers because of the amount of coal needed.

Liner design and the power of their engines began to improve greatly in the mid 1850s. Their builders owed a great deal to Brunel. In 1845 he finished the *Great Britain*. It was ninety-six metres long, and they were ninety-six metres of iron. Iron may be heavier than wood but it is much stronger so less structure is needed which means an iron ship can carry twice its own weight. Instead of paddles the *Great Britain* had a screw propellor at the rear. The first propellor-driven ship had been launched in 1838. Brunel had seen the possibilities and arranged a tug of war between her and a similar ship fitted with paddles. The propellor driven boat had dragged the other through the water.

The *Great Britain* made four round trips to New York before she ran aground over rocks in northern Ireland (because no-one had foreseen that the compass would be affected by the iron in the hull). Any other ship would have broken up. The great iron girders of the *Great Britain* meant she was no more than dented. It was an important lesson to ship-builders.

Brunel's last work was on an even grander scale. The frontiers of the shipping business were shifting to the longest run of all – to Australia. Huge sailing ships went there to bring back wool and often took emigrants on the way out. A few steamships had made the journey but had needed to stop at Capetown to take on coal specially shipped out from Wales.

Brunel built the *Great Eastern* to make this journey without refuelling. She was 207 metres long and had both a screw propellor and paddles. Brunel died eight days after she was launched and never knew that the *Great Eastern* did not succeed as the great ocean liner he had planned. She was too large for any company to want to buy her. Only later did she come into her own when she was found to be the only ship in the world which could carry the weight of cables needed to lay a line between Britain and America in 1866.

Contrasts in travel

Ocean-going steamers were the most exciting development in shipping in the mid-nineteenth century. Their owners made a great show of the luxury they offered in private cabins and lavish dining saloons. But conditions were not typical. Many more sailing ships than steamers crossed the Atlantic until the late nineteenth century.

As the wealthy transferred to steam, sailing ships began to deal more in steerage passengers crammed together between decks. In the late 1840s and the 1850s many hundreds of thousands of emigrants travelled steerage to America. Most were Irish moving away from Ireland after the great famine caused by the potato blight.

A **Contrasts**

A2 Below decks on a ship carrying emigrants to north America.

A1 The Grand Saloon of the *Great Britain*, 1852.

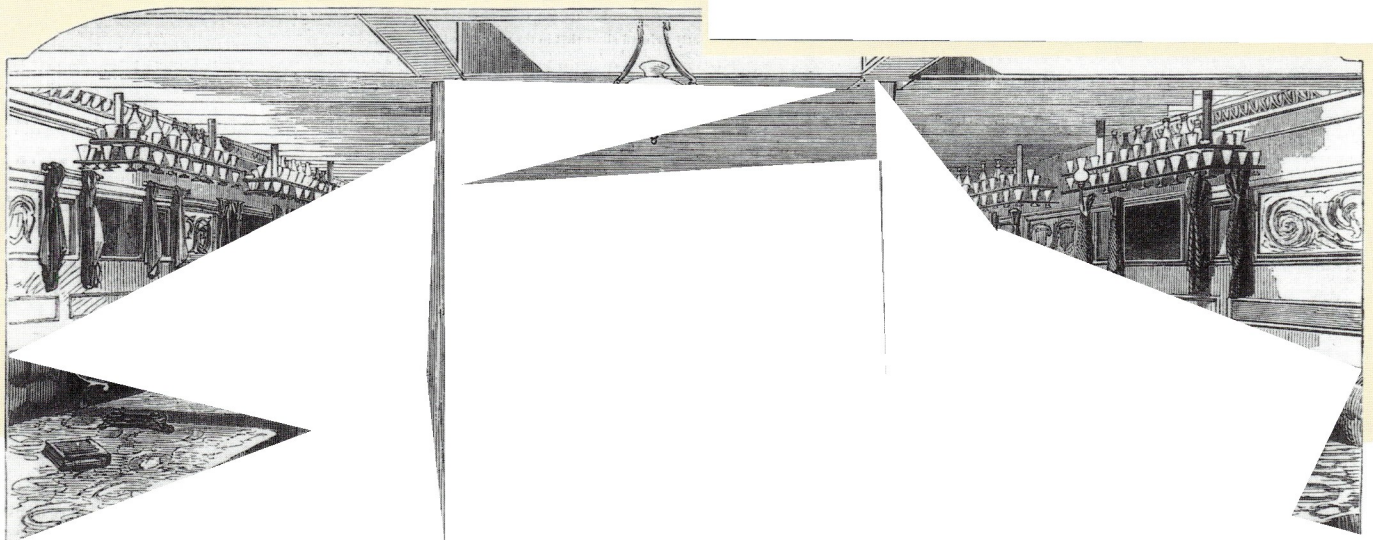

C SKILLS SECTION

Reliving the experience

A

A cabin passenger on the Australia run, 1840.

...the first pig was killed Saturday last, children had a roast of it on Sunday with which they were delighted...it was as delicate as lamb, so different from the pork on shore...We are to have a sheep and pig killed every week, the pigs are very small; we have good soup every day and the children the same and fresh meat every week.

Quoted in B Greenhill and A Gifford, *Women under Sail*, David and Charles, 1970

B

A steerage passenger on the Atlantic run, 1848.

...our provisions are delivered to us from the store rooms on Mondays and Thursdays and our water every morning. This morning it was taken from a fresh cask, and it stank so that we could not drink it, so we were obliged to boil it and put peppermint with it...

The provisions we took with us we have found most useful, such as flour as we can bake household bread every three days if we like for 1d a loaf; also a pie or pudding at ½d each. There is an excellent cast-iron oven and Boiler in the Galley...our sea biscuits contain so much horse bean flour, and our water is so impure that it produced indigestion.

Quoted in B Greenhill and A Gifford, *Travelling by sea in the nineteenth century*, A & C Black, 1972

1. What clues do these two passages give you about the difference in services offered to cabin and steerage passengers?

C

A storm in the Atlantic in the early 1850s. A captain's account.

Two days out of our home port we encountered the makings of a full gale and the ship was caught abeam by a heavy sea...the sails bellied and crashed and were finally ripped to shreds ...When at last we ran clear of bad weather, we made new sails, refitted the stateroom galley and my passengers sat down to their first hot meal for five days.

I was forced to keep my three hundred and seventy-five steerage passengers, men, women and children, under hatches. Many of them exhausted their food supplies before the ship made port and I felt great pity for the poor souls. The weather easing, I ordered hatches to be raised, and as they were fierce clouds of steam arose in the cold air and the resulting stench might well have come from a pig-stye...Before the ship made port five babies were born among the emigrants, the mothers attended in labour by the carpenter, a resourceful man, whose duties included the pulling of teeth among the ailing emigrants.

Quoted in P Brophy, *Sailing ships*, Hamlyn, 1974

2. List the ways in which this passage a) confirms the information in A and B, and b) adds to it.
3. What were your reactions on reading Source C? Do you think they would have been the same as someone reading it in the 1850s?

Knowledge and understanding

1. List the arguments you would make in support of the statement that port building was one of the essential features of the industrial revolution.

2. Explain why most freight was carried on sailing ships in the 1850s.

3. Using the rest of this book, make notes to show how the post service was important in encouraging transport developments from about 1700 to about 1850.

A SOURCE MISCELLANY

Advertisements

A

A1 Pickfords.

twenty, remarkably fine, powerful, fresh, good-actioned, short-legged horses in beautiful condition . . . just taken off their well-known, London–Manchester van in consequence of the intended opening of the railroad from Liverpool to London.

14 June 1837

A2 The beginnings of electric telegraphs, 1845.

Under the Special Patronage of Her Majesty

And H. R. H. Prince Albert

GALVANIC AND MAGNETO
ELECTRIC TELEGRAPH,
GT. WESTERN RAILWAY.

The Public are respectfully informed that this interesting & most extraordinary Apparatus, by which upwards of 50 SIGNALS can be transmitted to a Distance of 280,000 MILES in ONE MINUTE,

May be seen in operation, daily, (Sundays excepted,) from 9 till 8, at the

Telegraph Office, Paddington,
AND TELEGRAPH COTTAGE, SLOUGH.

ADMISSION 1s.

"This Exhibition is well worthy a visit from all who love to see the wonders of science."—MORNING POST.

Despatches instantaneously sent to and fro with the most confiding secrecy. Post Horses and Conveyances of every description may be ordered by the ELECTRIC TELEGRAPH, to be in readiness on the arrival of a Train, at either Paddington or Slough Station.

The Terms for sending a Despatch, ordering Post Horses, &c., only One Shilling.

N.B. Messengers in constant attendance, so that communications received by Telegraph, would be forwarded, if required, to any part of London, Windsor, Eton, &c.

THOMAS HOME, *Licensee.*

G. NURTON, Printer, 48, Church Street, Portman Market.

STEAM.
FOR LONDON,
Calling off YARMOUTH and SCARBRO', each Way, Weather permitting.
THE
KING of THE NETHERLANDS

Leaves NEWCASTLE.	SHIELDS.	SUNDERLAND.
JUNE.		
Saturday Afternoon, 2nd — at 5 o'Clock.	6 o'Clock.	7 o'Clock.
Saturday Afternoon, 9th — 1 —	2 —	3 —
Saturday Afternoon, 16th — 5 —	6 —	7 —
Saturday Morning, 23rd — 11 —	12 —	1 —
Saturday Afternoon, 30th — 5 —	6 —	7 —
JULY.		
Saturday Morning, 7th — 11 —	12 —	1 —
Saturday Afternoon, 14th — 4 —	5 —	6 —
Saturday Evening, 21st — 8 —	9 —	10 —
Saturday Afternoon, 28th — 4 —	5 —	6 —
AUGUST.		
Saturday Evening, 4th — 7 —	8 —	9 —
Saturday Afternoon, 11th — 3 —	4 —	5 —
Saturday Evening, 18th — 6 —	7 —	8 —
Saturday Afternoon, 25th — 3 —	4 —	5 —

The Times of sailing will be regularly published in the above Manner, during the Season.

FARES, *including Provisions of the best Quality.*

NEWCASTLE to LONDON, ... Best Cabin, ... **£3.**	Fore Cabin, **£2.**	
Ditto SCARBRO'...... Ditto ... — .... **£1. 1s.**	Ditto, ...	**15s.**
Ditto YARMOUTH, Ditto, ... **£2.**	Ditto, ... **£1. 7s.**	

Children under 10 Years of Age, Half-Price.

GOODS AT MODERATE RATES.
TEAS, 2s. PER CHEST.

Parcels, 2s 3s. or 4s, according to Size or Weight. Four-wheeled Carriages, £6. 6s. Two-wheeled do. £4. 4s Horses, without Food, £4. 4s. Dogs, with Food, 10s

Passengers, by the King of the Netherlands embark and disembark at the Company's Wharf, Entrance of the West India Docks, Blackwall, free of Expense, and without the use of small Boats.

AGENTS. { ALEXANDER MITCHELL, 35, *Leadenhall Street*, London, JOSEPH SHIELD & Co., 50, *Quayside*, and *Folly Wharf, Newcastle*.

All Goods must be delivered at the Folly Wharf, Two Hours previous to the Vessel starting.

THE KING OF THE NETHERLANDS

Leaves **London** for **Newcastle** every Wednesday Morning Ten o'Clock.

FOR LEITH,
THE ARDINCAPLE,
Captain Mowbray,

Leaves NEWCASTLE every *Monday and Friday Morning* at 6, and SHIELDS at 7.
Leaves LEITH for NEWCASTLE every *Wednesday Morning* at 7, and every *Saturday Evening* at 6

FARES, without Provisions.

Best Cabin, ...	15s.
Second Cabin, ...	10s.

Children under 10 Years of Age, Half-Price.

☞ Refreshments may be had of the Steward at moderate Rates.

Having now a Hold appropriated for Goods, LIGHT GOODS at the same Rate as the Sailing Vessels.

WHARFINGERS. { JOSEPH SHIELD, *Folly Wharf, Newcastle,* JAMES PEARSON, 10, *Shore, Leith.*

All Goods for Leith, to be delivered at the Folly Wharf, by 6 o'Clock the Evening previous to the Packet sailing.

N. B. Regular Trading Vessels to GAINSBRO', HULL, GLASGOW, BERWICK, DUNDEE, LIVERPOOL, and BRISTOL.

Folly Wharf, Newcastle, 28th May, 1832.

W. BOAG, PRINTER, NEWCASTLE.

A3 A shipping company in 1832.

1. What does A1 tell you about an effect of the coming of railways?
2. What was the connection between A2 and railways?
3. Why were services like that in A3 popular?

Scenes

Stourport, painted in 1776.

4. Why was a new town growing here?
5. Add notes to the picture to explain what can be seen and why it is important in transport history.

Vehicles

C

C1   A waggonway, 1727.

C2   A carrier's waggon, 1801.

6. What material was the rail in C1 made of?
7. Explain the shape of the wheels in C2.
8. Write brief notes to explain how each of these drawings illustrates an important development in transport history.

Two historians

D

D1

For many ages, and to the middle of this century, a causeway, about two feet broad, paved with round pebbles, was all that man or horse could travel upon, particularly in the winter season, through both Lancashire and Cheshire. This causeway was guarded by posts at a proper distance to keep carts off it, and the open part of the road was generally impassable in the winter from mire and deep ruts. As trade increased, turnpikes became general, and the ruts were filled up with pebbles and cinders, but still, in winter, no coach or chaise [dared] venture through them . . . lawsuits produced broad pavements, which would suffer two carriages to pass each other and this was thought perfection. In this state the roads continued many years, but now both the broad and the narrow paths are filling up, the pebble broken into small pieces, and the interstices [spaces] filled up with sand.

Adam Watkins, *Observations*, 1791

D2

The chief improvement made of late years in England in regard to turnpike roads, has consisted in reconstructing them upon more scientific principles than were previously employed, an advantage which is mainly owing to the exertions of the late Mr. McAdam, whose plans have been adopted generally throughout the kingdom, as well as in several foreign countries.

G.R. Porter, *Progress of the Nation*, 1851

9. From source D1, explain what a causeway was.
10. How does D1 explain a) why turnpikes were important, and b) the main weaknesses in their work.
11. Expain the connection between the complaints made by Adam Watkins and the developments described by G.R. Porter.